Voices of Internally Displaced Persons in Kenya

A Human Rights Perspective

Voices of Internally Displaced Persons in Kenya
A Human Rights Perspective

Roseanne Njiru & Bandana Purkayastha

frontpage

frontpage
www.frontpagepublications.com

First published 2015

Frontpage Publications Limited
Level 2, 13 John Prince's Street, London W1G 0JR, United Kingdom

Frontpage
Level B, 76 B B Ganguly Street, Kolkata 700012, India

British Library Cataloguing in Publishing Data
A catalogue record for this book is available from the British Library

ISBN: 978 93 81043 12 7

Printed in India
By Sadhana Udyog
76 B B Ganguly Street, Kolkata 700012, India

Typeset by Compuset International
85 Park Street, Kolkata 700016, India

Contents

Acknowledgement

We received a great deal of support during the course of this project. The passion and interest to theorise on the lives of IDPs in Kenya has been a long journey but it would not have been possible without the support of many individuals, institutions and agencies.

First, we are grateful to the Women's Empowerment Link (Kenya) and the then National Commission on Gender and Development (NCGD, now National Gender and Equality Commission) who introduced Roseanne Njiru into the world of IDPs through research on gender violence in the Kenya camps. Being part of the response efforts sparked her interest in the conditions and structural circumstances of IDPs. We have drawn a lot of insights from the research Njiru conducted at that time. Second, we acknowledge the help provided by the Human Rights Institute at the University of Connecticut for the summer 2012 graduate student research grant which enabled Njiru to conduct more research in the IDP camps in Kenya. Special thanks to the people that helped with the 2012 summer research; Allan Korongo of the University of Nairobi for helping with Swahili translations for the protocols and research instruments; Emmah Nungari then of the NCGD for the collaborative work we did in the camps over the years and support in this research; Ruth Ruraa and Lorrain Ombech who helped us gain access to various participants within government and civil society. Our gratitude goes out to these unnamed participants. Sincerest thanks to Amos Gathecha for the immense role he played in enabling Njiru access the camps. Thanks to Cythia Njeru for her help with transcriptions.

Roseanne is grateful to her academic advisor and mentor, Professor Bandana Purkayastha for pushing her into this book project making her graduate experience at UNCONN a stimulating and rewarding experience. Roseanne also thanks Professor Charles Nzioka of the University of Nairobi for his unfailing support. Many friends and colleagues were part of this process, including Farhan Yousaf, Adane Zawdu and Sheila Pierre. A special thanks to Chandra Waring for reading the typescripts and providing feedback.

We record our appreciation for the work of Abhijit Mazumder of Frontpage Publications but for whose commitment to social justice, this book would not have been written.

Bandana Purkayastha thanks friends and family members around the world for keeping her grounded in the important things in life.

Roseanne Njiru thanks her families for the support throughout this process. Roseanne's gratefulness to her son, Gary Wayne Shompah, for being ever so understanding and for reminding her to "work hard mom"; special gratitude to 'dad', Julius Shompah, for taking up the responsibility of bringing up the son enduring the mother's long absence. To her parents, siblings, nieces, nephews and friends, for being a pillar of support, Roseanne says, *Ngai amurathime muno!*

Most important, our gratitude goes to all the unnamed participants in this study without whose ungrudging support this project would not have seen light of day. We hope that the voices we 'picked' to represent the IDPs in Kenya adequately reflect their experiences and concerns. *Asante sana!*

Roseanne Njiru & Bandana Purkayastha
15 July 2014

Preface

We are preparing to publish this book at a time when the world is being torn apart (again) by vicious political, religious, inter-communal and other sectarian-induced conflicts. The United Nations High Commissioner for Refugees' (the UN's refugee agency) website is filled with 'urgent appeals' for donations to support fleeing victims of the crises in Syria, South Sudan, Central African Republic and Central Iraq. These human-created conflicts lead to physical injuries, sexual violence, psychological torture, destruction of homes, property and deaths, ultimately resulting in displacement of people who are often sheltered in camps. Camp life opens up another chapter of continued violence and different forms of human rights violations. This book reflects our deep concern for the lives of displaced men, women, girls and boys living in camps in Kenya who fled the politically instigated ethnic violence following the country's disputed elections in December 2007.

An immediate impetus for the book was Roseanne Njiru's earlier work with a Kenyan women's organisation in collaboration with other NGOs and government agencies to respond to gender violence in the camps. We ask: *why do* these violations continue in the camps that are set up to otherwise protect internally displaced persons (IDPs).

Thinking about protection, we realised that refugees are protected under an international convention while IDPs have no international legal framework for protection even though, in practice, they continue to experience human rights violations. Moreover, the UN Guiding Principles on Internal Displacement (UNGPID), unlike the framework for the protection of refugees, is not a legally binding international obligation. Given the practical challenges in enforcing protection of IDPs at the international human rights level, we find that IDPs are particularly vulnerable to human rights abuses in camps. Consequently, in this book, we examine the nexus of action by states, international bodies and NGOs and IDP's experiences.

One of the factors that leads to inadequate attention to human rights of IDPs is the perception of camps. From a political perspective, camps are seen as temporary spaces deserving minimum protection and provision of basic services, and sometimes the withdrawal of these services in order to facilitate resettlement. Yet, for the IDPs who have to live there for an indeterminate period of time, the camps are permanent places even in light of promises of resettlement. In our analysis, we link the lives of the men and women living in camps to the historical and contemporary socio-cultural and structural contexts in Kenya. Postcolonial Kenya's socio-economic and political realities – ethnic relations, land redistribution and allocation of resources, gendered structures and transformation of roles, and governance – are shaped by traces of colonialism and contemporary neo-colonialism and global capitalism. These politics continued to shape human rights in camps and derailed resettlement and restoration of dignity and as a sequel, gendered violence and other human rights abuses were evident before, during and after the conflict situation.

Finally, we note that as we were preparing this book, the government "officially" declared that there were no more IDPs resulting from the post-election violence in the country. However, as we conducted this research, analysed NGO and newspaper reports, and watched news on television, critical concerns with creating more camp-like conditions post-resettlement were raised. We have argued that simple moves out of camps do not enable people to access human rights and build lives of human dignity if social and structural circumstances are not addressed and adequate protection measures are put in place. Consequently, we also suggest future research on resettlement and human dignity.

CHAPTER ONE

Introduction

Our main problem here is health; it is hard to find food, health care. Even when a person dies, it is difficult to bury them. Life here is hard. We have nothing we can say is okay. We have this place to sleep but you can see the compound, our diet. Generally, our life is bad. Let me say I left my home with no health problems but now I am always being rushed to hospital as if I am dying. How many people have died here, how many are lying in bed sick? They are many. Yet the government is now calm. Like now, if you go to tell them that you have lost a family member (family member died), they will ask "what kind of person? IDP?" I would like them to stop politicising IDP issues. They should know we are *human. They should ask themselves, what if they were like us. I am now sick and I was not sick before the violence (Married female, 66 years).*

My husband beat me up because I refused to have sex with him. He came back home at night drunk and was loudly demanding for sex in the presence of the children. Our tents are very small and we have three children but he still wants me to have sex. Some couples quarrel until they throw each other out of their tents like my neighbours did (Married female, 45 years).

> *I know a young girl here, she has three children. These young girls and men are idle because they cannot find work. This place is like a town (prostitution). They do it day and night, in the maize field and the abandoned airstrip; there is no need for lodging (Widowed female, 50 years).*

> *There is poor security here. I was attacked and all my things stolen. I am asking if you people (interviewer) can help me with a tent since mine was stolen. I went to the DO (District Officer) and the chief but nobody has helped me. During the attack, I lost my teeth and my hand was cut off. I am helpless (Married male, 30 years).*

> *I think men are oppressed and women do not listen to us anymore. As her husband, if she refuses to listen, we will probably quarrel or I will beat her otherwise I will not sleep (Married male, 32 years).*

> *It is as if it is against the rules of this camp to talk about love. You have to organise and go elsewhere, so we meet at the cemetery where there is peace and no disturbance. But the girls in the camp ignore us because we are broke, so they go outside (have sex with men outside the camp) (Single male, 20 years).*

These voices of internally displaced persons (IDPs) in Kenya draw our attention to various forms of human rights abuses that women and men of varying ages experienced in the IDP camps following the 2007-08 post-election violence. Sadly, these experiences are not unique or surprising in conflict situations. There is a large literature on the situation of war and conflict in Africa, particularly focusing on gender violence (for example, Eriksson Baaz and Stern 2013; Meintjes, Pillay and Turshen 2002; Moser and Clark 2001; Prescott and Madsen 2011; Turshen 1988, 2000; Turshen and Alidou 2000; Turshen and Twagiramariya 1998). Kenya, however, has largely been considered a relatively stable country on the continent with only a history of "small scale" ethnic election conflicts since multi-party democracy in 1991. Indeed, Kenya hosts many refugees from neighbouring war-torn countries, especially Somalia, Sudan and Ethiopia. It also acts as a regional headquarters to many international government and non-governmental agencies that provide services to neighbouring countries in situations of conflict. The conflicts following the December 2007 presidential elections in Kenya, therefore, came as a surprise to many people.

Scholarly literature on Kenya suggests that ethnic conflicts that have surfaced in the country's elections since the introduction of multipartyism are rooted in pre-election political campaigns to intimidate certain ethnic groups from voting; factors such as unequal access to land (and in effect, economic inequality) (Kanyinga 1981, 2001; Klopp 2001; Okoth-Ogendo 1981) and the rise of militia groups (Oloo 2010) are also identified as factors that shaped ethnic political clashes in Kenya. Moreover, seemingly there is no significant attempt, especially from the political scientists, to examine what happens to people who seek shelter from violence in camps for IDPs. Very little investigation has been made into the ability of IDPs to access human rights in the camps created to specifically protect them. Moreover, the scholarly emphasis on political and economic (land) issues as separate, instead of intersecting, also limits our understanding of how social, economic, cultural and political factors work together to shape human rights abuses for internally displaced populations in Kenya.

Dukes (1999) points out that social and political institutions set the context for individual and group behaviour and are meant to provide the resources individuals need to survive. The way in which people act and live is in part shaped by the social structures in which they find themselves. Therefore, the social justice project, which includes understanding and valuing human rights, is partly about ensuring that these structures and institutions, in reality, do satisfy people's basic human needs and their ability to live lives of human dignity. Arden (1999) additionally argues that where these institutions are characterised by exploitation, political exclusion, and unequal access to resources, these structural forces often create a system in which people become trapped in particular debilitating social situations. Structural violence, therefore, often results in, and exacerbates existing inequalities of power, creates poverty, and leads to the denial of basic human rights (Dukes 1999). Such inequalities of power, economic conditions, and access to rights that arise from these structural arrangements often cause protracted and intractable conflicts (Maiese 2003).

In this critique, we examine the 2007-08 election violence in Kenya that, unlike previously reported electoral conflicts, took place immediately after the presidential election results were announced on 30 December 2007. We analyse the accounts of men and women who live in camps that were set up following the violence. We draw upon scholarly approaches that have emphasised a continuum of violence, spanning within intimate spheres, engendered through a variety of local to international conflicts. We further use a human rights perspective to emphasise violence as a human rights issue, to bring into focus the social structural contexts that lead to violence and how the structural contexts within camps create vulnerabilities to other forms of violence. Specifically, we describe what happens to people who flee violence and why they remain vulnerable in camps that are meant to protect them from violence.

In the book, we focus on Kenya as an empirical case study of internal displacement and human right violations in order to provide further impetus to the growing academic debate on internally displaced populations globally, especially those displaced through intra-country political conflicts. Although we are analysing internal displacement in Kenya, our focus is on persons who were displaced after the post-election violence. There have been other displacements prior to and after this period as a result of evictions from government reserve lands, political ethnic tensions, or natural disasters. Since our field data covers post 2007 election violence only, there is no endeavour to offer any comprehensive understanding between political conflicts and other displacements in Kenya. Our analysis draws upon – and problematises – our knowledge of politically instigated conflicts in Kenya, but goes beyond Kenya as a case (Eriksson Baaz and Stern 2013). Election violence and violence that leads to displacements, in general, have grown rapidly in many countries. Some of the insights in this book are, therefore, relevant for understanding and framing human rights abuses for internally displaced persons beyond Kenya that have similar structural circumstances. Before we delve any further into human rights issues, we turn to defining internally displaced persons as they are distinguished from refugees in international human rights legal frameworks and practice.

WHO IS AN INTERNALLY DISPLACED PERSON?

The issue of internal displacement emerged into the international agenda in the early 1990s. At this point, no definition of "internally displaced persons" existed. Yet, in order to assist them, it was important that there be an agreed term for identifying this group to compile data, frame laws and policies (Mooney 2005). According to Phuong (2004), the early definition of IDPs was a negative one. IDPs were initially defined as people who had fled their homes but were not refugees. In 1992, the Representative of UN Secretary-General on IDPs had, however, proposed a working definition that considered two basic criteria of internal displacement: (a) the involuntary nature of the movement and (b) that the movement takes place within the national borders (Mooney 2005). The second element of this definition distinguishes an internally displaced person from a refugee who, the 1951 Refugee Convention defines as being outside the country of his/her nationality.[1] The UN Secretary-General thus defined IDPs as:

> Persons or groups who have been forced to flee their homes suddenly or unexpectedly in large numbers, as a result of armed conflict, internal strife, systematic violations of human rights or natural or man-made disaster, and who are within the territory of their own country.

According to Mooney (2005), this definition was broad enough to take into account the various circumstances in which people become displaced, but it was too narrow, particularly in its temporal and numerical criteria. For example, it limited the IDPs only to those who fled their homes "suddenly or unexpectedly" overlooking the ways in which displacement could be an organised state policy such as in Burma, Ethiopia or Iraq. Also the use of "forced to flee" would exclude all those situations where populations did not flee but were obliged to leave their homes, for instance, the forced evictions of minorities during the war in Bosnia (Mooney 2005). There was also the issue of people fleeing 'in large numbers'. This would, however, exclude people who fled in small groups or individually.[2] This definition was thus comprehensively revised as contained in the 1998 United Nations Guiding Principles on Internal Displacement (UNGPID) as:

> Persons or groups of persons who have been forced or obliged to flee or to leave their homes or places of habitual residence, in particular as a result of or in order to avoid the effects of armed conflict, situations of generalised violence, violations of human rights or natural or human-made disasters, and who have not crossed an internationally recognised State border.

Phuong (2004) points out that while not defined as refugees, IDPs[3] have, however, been dealt with by refugee structures such as UNHCR providing protection and assistance to them. Nonetheless, she notes that internal displacement is linked with the refugee problem in so far as it often constitutes a preliminary step towards external displacement, but the phenomenon also has other specific characteristics. For example, the sensitivity of linking the IDP issue with the willingness of refugee-receiving states to contain refugee flow within the countries of origin. Phuong argues that while asserting humanitarian motives, these states may focus on in-country protection simply to prevent their asylum obligations from being activated. By preventing border crossing of the populations necessary to activate the obligations contained in the 1951 Conventions, states by and large avoid these obligations. According to Phuong, therefore, the increase in the concern for IDPs can be explained by two reasons of varied nature: (a) humanitarian, and (b) the other having more political and self-serving overtone to prevent IDPs from becoming refugees. Importantly, Phuong, quoting Adelman (2003), has pointed out that researchers need to unpack concepts, policies and justifications used by the political actors when they define IDPs and develop mechanisms to offer them assistance. In keeping with this line of scholarship, we also emphasise that the theoretical and conceptual discussions on the politics of defining IDPs, and debates on shifting responsibilities between states and the UN agencies are critical because they have a bearing on the kinds and processes of protections offered to them. We will refer to the human rights implications of the definition and categorisation of IDPs when we deal with the principles under which internally displaced people are protected.

In the next section, we provide a brief summary of the growing global phenomenon of IDPs in the last few years in order to situate IDPs within the global context of displacement.

GLOBAL OVERVIEW OF INTERNAL DISPLACEMENT

Internal displacement remains one of the world's most significant human rights and humanitarian challenges, as millions of people continue to be internally displaced every year. Like refugees, IDPs are forcibly displaced by conflict, generalised violence and human rights violations. IDPs may also be displaced by natural disasters and development projects. According to the Geneva-based Internal Displacement Monitoring Centre (IDMC 2013), about two-thirds of the world's forcibly uprooted people are displaced within their own countries. IDMC's statistics on displacement – which focus only on persons displaced by armed conflict, generalised violence and/or human rights violations – show that the global number of IDPs has grown steadily in the last few years from a total of around 17 million in 1997. At the end of 2006, it was estimated that there were 24.5 million IDPs in some 52 countries; Africa had the largest IDP population, with around 11.8 million in 21 countries (IDMC 2007). The latest 2013 figures indicate that there were approximately 28.8 million IDPs around the world in 2012, up from 26.4 million in 2011. Over 6.5 million people were newly displaced inside their home countries in 2012, almost twice as many as compared to the previous year. The report indicates that the conflicts in Syria and the Democratic Republic of the Congo (DRC), with the figures standing at 2.4 million and one million respectively, were responsible for most of the new displacements while an estimated 500,000 people fled their homes in both Sudan and India.

The regions with the largest increase in the number of IDPs in 2012 were the Middle East and North Africa, where 2.5 million people were forced to flee their homes. There were almost 6 million IDPs in the regions at the end of 2012, a rise of 40 per cent on the 2011 number. The figure continued to rise in 2013. Asia had the second highest increase in new displacements with 1.4 million people forced to flee their homes during 2012. Overall, the region with the largest total number of IDPs was sub-Saharan Africa hosting 10.4 million, an increase of 7.5 per cent compared with the year before, thus reversing the downward trend recorded since 2004. Africa's displaced population accounts for almost a third of the global total. The year 2012 has been labelled as the continent's worst year for violent conflict. The America region hosted the second largest number of IDPs in 2012 with a total of 5.8 million, an increase of 3 per cent. Colombia remains the country with the highest number of IDPs in the world, with a total of between 4.9 and 5.5 million, according to the IDMC. The country's internal armed conflict forced an estimated 230,000 people to flee their homes during the year. Statistics on displacement show that between 70 and 80 per cent of all IDPs are women and children (IDMC 2006).

It must be noted that it is difficult to provide an accurate figure on IDPs since the numbers fluctuate for various reasons. First, some IDPs flee to urban centres or cities or flee to their relatives' homes. Second, IDPs are on the move – some IDPs may be returning home through resettlement programmes while others are fleeing – so it becomes challenging to provide statistics that would depict a comprehensive picture. Third, some IDPs periodically go back to the camps to take advantage of humanitarian and/or government support further complicating the process through which IDPs are estimated; and finally, most official figures would only include those displaced by conflict or natural disasters. Development-induced IDPs often are not included in assessments (IDMC 2006). Given these, the global statistics on IDPs are an approximation because they are often a subject for debate among different humanitarian, developmental and governmental organisations. For example, they may rely on head counts in camps at a particular time thus leaving out those not residing in camps but yet displaced (Personal conversation with Kenyan government official).

By the end of 2012, UNHCR, the UN refugee agency, was looking after approximately 15.5 million IDPs, more than the total number of refugees of concern to the agency. Important to note is that UNHCR only assists IDPs as part of a wider intervention by the international community since there is no international legal framework for protecting the IDPs who, ironically, outnumber refugees today. By definition, IDPs have not crossed an international border thus, they remain legally under the protection of their own government – even though that government may be the cause of their plight. As citizens, the IDPs retain all of their rights and protection under both human rights and international humanitarian law (United Nations High Commission for Refugees 2012).

What this brief overview and the figures presented above suggest is that a large number of people are vulnerable to human rights abuses in spite of the existence of various human rights frameworks in their countries. In addition, the gendered dynamic in displacement (70-80 per cent constitute women and children) indicates the likelihood of their gender/ age-specific vulnerabilities. Even more important, the fact that IDPs may flee as a result of state human rights violations begs the question of the commitment of the same governments in protecting and safeguarding the rights of IDPs. Unlike refugees who have an international legal framework of protection, (even though in practice the Refugee Convention safeguards may be limited), IDPs largely remain at the mercy of their governments. As the next section indicates, the assumption that other international and domestic human rights instruments may be adequate for the protection of the IDPs is, at best, misplaced.

INTERNATIONAL HUMAN RIGHTS STANDARDS AND IDPS

The movement of people fleeing from armed conflict, wars and various forms of persecution in search of safety is an age-old phenomenon. It was, however, not until the 20th Century that universal standards for the protection of such people were developed. Since the establishment of the League of Nations after the end of World War I, the international protection of people in conflict situations has evolved over the years and much has been written about conceptual, legal and institutional challenges that have contributed to this evolution (Majodina 2009). The United Nations took the lead in developing an international 'bill of rights' that laid the groundwork for further elaboration of protection mechanisms under international human rights law. The Bill of Rights consists of the Universal Declaration of Human Rights (UDHR 1948), the International Covenant on Civil and Political Rights (ICCPR 1966) and the International Covenant on Economic, Social and Cultural Rights (ICESCR 1966).

The UDHR spells out the fundamental human rights. Article 2 of the UDHR partly states that, "Everyone is entitled to all the rights and freedoms set forth in this Declaration, without distinction of any kind, such as race, colour, sex, language, religion, political or other opinion, national or social origin, property, birth or other status", implying that human rights are universal, inalienable and indivisible, shared equally by everyone (Ishay 2004, Omara Otunnu et al 2012). Broadly, the ICCPR commits parties to respect the civil and political rights of individuals including the right to life, self-determination, and electoral rights, among others. The ICESCR, on the other hand, lists several rights that states should introduce to ensure decent lives for their people. These include labour rights, right to social security, health, education, and decent living. Specifically, article 11 recognises the right of everyone to an adequate standard of living, which includes the right to adequate food, housing, and clothing.

In addition to this, the Convention on the Elimination of All Forms of Discrimination against Women (CEDAW), adopted in 1979 by the UN General Assembly, is often described as an international bill of rights for women. It defines what constitutes discrimination against women and sets up an agenda for national action to put an end to such discrimination. CEDAW addresses issues such as ensuring women's equal access to, and equal opportunities in political and public life – including the right to vote and to stand for election – as well as education, health, employment, and reproductive rights. State parties agree to take all appropriate measures, including legislation and temporary special measures so that women can enjoy all their human rights and fundamental freedoms. In spite of attempting to raise consciousness on multiple discriminations that affect women, CEDAW does not particularly address violence against women.

Therefore, global activism by women spelt out limitations of these earlier treaties and conventions in addressing violence against women leading to the 1993 UN Declaration of Elimination of Violence against Women that defined VAW as "any act of gender-based violence that results in, or is likely to result in, physical, sexual or mental harm or suffering to women, including threats of such acts, coercion or arbitrary deprivation of liberty, whether occurring in public or in private life" (United Nations 1993) to highlight a continuum of VAW from the family spheres to communities and to violence perpetrated by the state (Erturk and Purkayastha 2012).

Lomo (2000) has argued that the existing international legal framework provides sufficient protection to everyone, including victims of forced migration, both refugees and IDPs. He, however, points out several factors that impede this protection, some of which include: the lack of political will to use the available legal mechanisms in a way that can optimally protect both refugees and IDPs; state failure to enact laws necessary or to create the institutional frameworks to give effect to the international human rights protection regime; impoverishment and lack of information about rights for people living in sub-Saharan Africa making them amenable to manipulation, sectarianism and coercion; and that the geo-political and economic interests of some states directly impact how the body of human rights law is implemented or interpreted.

Our view coincides with that of Lomo's, that at the international level, the human rights frameworks are envisioned as edifices to protect and preserve the dignity of all human beings including those fleeing from conflict and wars. We would, however, point out that a major assumption of the frameworks is that people are in stable conditions where they can access and claim these rights. When people are dislocated through war, political conflicts, ethnic tensions, and natural disasters, the accessibility and ability to claim these rights often comes into question. Further, it is even more difficult to claim rights if the state and/or the political elite are responsible for such dislocation.

As we noted in the previous section, the view that international standards and (other domestic laws) are adequate for protection of all citizens collapses when we consider the case of people fleeing politically instigated conflicts within countries. Thus, as a result of the recognition of the special vulnerabilities of IDPs, UN agencies have developed a set of guiding principles which, unlike the framework for the protection of refugees, is not a legally binding international obligation, creating, consequently, practical challenges in enforcement and implementation of these principles.

THE GUIDING PRINCIPLES ON INTERNAL DISPLACEMENT (UNGPID)

We have noted above that most of the international human rights standards assume a stable context in which people are able to make claims of their rights thus excluding vulnerable populations such as the IDPs and refugees. The 1951 Refugee Convention and its 1967 Protocol were developed as a result of recognising the extreme vulnerability of refugees to human rights abuses. Unlike refugees, there is, however, no specific international law for the protection of IDPs despite their rising numbers. Since IDPs have not crossed any recognised state border, the existing international law applied to refugees cannot be drawn upon to respond to IDPs.

Consequently, in response to the growing phenomena of IDPs worldwide, the international community – specifically the United Nations – began to focus formally on promoting the rights and needs of the internally displaced. In 1992, the UN Secretary-General, at the behest of the UN Commission on Human Rights, appointed Dr Francis M Deng as the Representative of Internally Displaced Persons. This process culminated in the development of a normative framework specifically tailored to address and meet the needs of IDPs: The Guiding Principles on Internal Displacement (UNGPID) in 1998. The UNGPID contains 30 guiding principles drawn from international human rights law, international humanitarian law, and the international refugee law. They identify rights and guarantees relevant to protection from forced displacement, protection and assistance during displacement and the process of resettlement and reintegration (Kenya Human Rights Commission 2009). It was hoped that, though nonbinding, the document would provide authoritative guidance to states and all other authorities, groups and persons in their relationship with IDPs.

The guiding principles have gained international recognition as the key international framework for the protection of internally displaced persons. According to Walter Kälin (2010), the Representative of the Secretary-General on the Human Rights of IDPs, at regional and sub-regional levels, the adoption of the African Union Convention for the Protection and Assistance of Internally Displaced Persons in Africa (Kampala Convention) and the IDP Protocol of the Pact on Security, Stability and Development in the Great Lakes Region[4] (the Great Lakes Pact) are breakthrough measures towards binding international law. Moreover, increasingly, many countries, especially those that have experienced high numbers of displacements, have developed or are in the process of developing domestic laws and policies based on the Guiding Principles. These include Chad, Nepal, Central African Republic, Turkey, and Yemen (Kälin 2010). Kenya began the process of formulating a policy on internal displacement after the 2007-08 election conflicts even though there were other displacements before this.

Nonetheless, we note that while a strong normative framework is a necessary condition for the protection of human rights of the IDPs, it remains insufficient as long as its implementation is weak. Therefore, despite the increased thinking at the international, regional and national levels about how to deal with IDPs through development of legal frameworks specific to protection of displaced persons, in practice not enough attention has been paid to ensure the dignity of people living in camps through existing legal frameworks that guarantee the rights of every human being. Subsequently, IDPs in every region continue to face a range of risks including threats to their physical security and integrity, gender violence, discrimination, lack of access to basic necessities (such as food, clothing, health, shelter), livelihoods, and violation of their rights relating to land and property. This, of course, occurs despite the existence of the UNGPID, in addition to other international, regional and domestics human rights frameworks.

As previous research on refugees and IDPs has shown, the development of rights frameworks for vulnerable populations does not, therefore, guarantee protection if there is lack of political will in implementation. Whether people in vulnerable situations have the ability and opportunity to make claims of their rights still remains a question. Furthermore, specific populations – women, children – experience displacement in devastating ways that arise from their social structural locations. In order to trace some responses to the question about human rights of IDPs, we first turn to a specific context, Kenya, and look at the various international rights standards and some of the domestic laws that exist in the country.

HUMAN RIGHTS STANDARDS IN KENYA

Kenya provides a good context for understanding the particular challenges of internal displacement, especially so because Kenya has indeed ratified many international and regional human rights instruments. At the international level, Kenya is party to: International Covenant on Civil and Political Rights (ICCPR); International Covenant on Economic, Social and Cultural Rights (ICESCR); International Convention on the Elimination of All Forms of Racial Discrimination (ICERD); Convention on the Elimination of All Forms of Discrimination against Women (CEDAW); Convention against Torture and other Cruel, Inhuman or Degrading Treatment or Punishment; Convention on the Rights of the Child (CRC); Optional Protocol to Convention on the Rights of the Child on the sale of Children, Child Prostitution and Child Pornography;

Convention on the Non-applicability of Statutory Limitation to War Crimes and Crimes against Humanity; International Convention against Corruption; Convention Relating to the Status of Refugees; Rome Statute of the International Criminal Court; and Forty-nine ILO Conventions, with 43 of them in force. At the African regional level, Kenya is signatory to, among others, The African Charter on Human and Peoples' Rights; The African Charter on the Rights and Welfare of the Child; The Great Lakes protocol on the protection and Assistance of IDPs; The OAU Convention Governing Specific Aspects of Refugee Problems in Africa; The OAU Convention Against Corruption (Human Rights Committee 2010). But, the most important question is, how have these international and regional legal instruments interacted with national human rights systems?

Prior to the promulgation of the Constitution of Kenya in August 2010, international treaties were not considered as part of Kenyan laws. Therefore, they could not be directly applied by the courts, tribunals or administrative authorities in the absence of domestic legislation reflecting the same objectives and principles. Nonetheless, some courts have interpreted the laws of Kenya so they were not in conflict with treaties to which Kenya is a party. After the post-election violence in 2007-08, the Kenya government could not be held accountable on the basis of ratification of these international instruments. Nonetheless, some instruments such as the Convention on the Rights of the Child and the African Charter on the Rights and Welfare of the Child had been legislated through the Children Act (Chapter 586 of the Laws of Kenya). Also, the Convention relating to the Status of Refugees and the OAU Convention Governing the Specific Aspects of Refugee Problems in Africa was enforced through the Refugees Act (No. 13 of 2006). Other international instruments such as the ICCPR, ICESCR, CEDAW, and ICERD had been domesticated through different legislations (Human Rights Committee 2010). The new Constitution changed this scenario substantiating that any treaty or convention ratified by Kenya shall form part of the law of Kenya, and the general rules of international law shall form part of the laws of Kenya. Though this seems problematic in light of social, cultural, economic and political context in Kenya, it provides a new environment in which the Kenyan state may be held accountable and answerable to human rights violations. It also means that the government would be challenged and find themselves in an awkward position to defend the lack of a policy on any human right violations, as was the case with the post-election violence. In that case, the government largely attributed the inadequate and untimely response to the violence victims to lack of a legal framework on internal displacement.

Since there was no legal mechanism for protection of IDPs when Kenya experienced the conflicts in 2007-08, they relied on the UNGPID and the Great Lakes Region (GLR) Protocol to respond to the violence. The GLR Protocol was developed in response to the social, economic and political consequences of the conflict situation in the region. The International Conference on the Great Lakes Region (IC/GLR) which began in 1999 led to the signing of a pact on security, stability and development in the Great Lakes Region in 2006. The Pact comprises 10 protocols, 3 of which are dedicated to IDPs: the protocol on the Protection and Assistance to IDPs; protocol on the Property Rights of the Returning Persons; and protocol on the Prevention and Suppression of Violence against Women and Children (Kenya Human Rights Commission 2009). Despite these normative frameworks, human rights organisations and scholars have criticised government responses to the violence (CREAW 2008; ICJ and KHRC 2009, 2012; KHRC 2008; Kamungi and Klopp 2007) while others have questioned the relevance of the IC/GLR (see Kamungi 2009). Nevertheless, they were important to the human rights activists because they drew on these protocols – in the absence of a domestic legal framework pertaining to IDPs – in advocating and lobbying for the rights of IDPs. It must be noted that

Kenya has an extremely vibrant human rights movement with significant international support. Despite various tensions with the government, the movement has managed to push for policy development and implementation, including the current IDP Act (2012) whose process began after the post-election violence.

It is important to record that Kenya recently developed a law for dealing with internal displacements, five years after the conflicts. The president assented to The *Prevention, Protection and Assistance to Internally Displaced Persons and Affected Communities Act* on 31 December 2012 which came into effect on 18 January 2013. The Act makes effective the UNGPID and IC/GLR Protocol that give specific guidelines on how to protect and manage IDPs. Some of the issues highlighted in the Act include a rights-based response to internal displacement; prevention and protection from displacement; assistance and protection after displacement. It is, however, important to note that lack of an effective national policy that members or their advocates can use to claim rights, coupled with lack of political goodwill to implement the policy may lead to discrepancies in the assistance provided to displaced persons. Since the enforcement of the IDP Act 2012, IDPs and human rights organisations hope that the government will adhere to the principles of the Act and humanely restore the dignity of displaced persons. More importantly, the Act gives more power to advocates and lobbyists to monitor and pressure the government to implement it.

To sum up on the international and domestic human rights standards for the protection of IDPs, we note that the international definition of different migrant populations has both legal and practical implications for their human rights. In the following section, we attempt to examine the implications of internal displacement within the intersection of migration and human rights to give a broader theoretical grounding of our analysis.

SITUATING INTERNAL DISPACEMENT WITHIN A MIGRATION AND HUMAN RIGHTS FRAMEWORK

As we have pointed out previously, when we consider the case of internally displaced persons we hit a conundrum. Refugees are protected under an international convention while IDPs have no international legal framework for their protection even though, in practice, these refugees continue to experience human rights violations. This international legal practice informs us that the human rights of a migrant are largely defined by the migration category to which she or he belongs and by the reasons behind the migration. As such, there is a continuum of various categories, ranging from the human rights of voluntary migrant workers and other economic migrants to refugees who are forced to leave their countries to escape persecution (Grant 2005). Conceptualised this way, we then find that migration and human rights are intersecting issues implying that there are human rights consequences for categorising and attributing legal status to some groups of migrants and not others, such as the IDPs.

Phuong (2005) in her work on the international protection of IDPs points out that internal displacement is a difficult subject for analysis because many of the standards for displacement are not part of the international law. For example, she notes that countries like China view situations causing internal displacement as falling within the domain of internal sovereignty and not an international concern. Many of the UN guiding principles on internal displacement have not been accepted by the international community either as customary practice or as treaty obligations. Phuong argues that internal displacement needs to be discussed within a wider human rights context. She, however, defends the need to distinguish between refugees and IDPs. In contrast, we argue that making distinctions between the two, within a framework of protection, is difficult and it might not make sense to draw the line between those who successfully cross state borders and those who do not. This is especially so because there are minimal protections for IDPs especially within the African region where there are inadequate resources for resettlement.

Many countries that are experiencing conflicts have poor governmental infrastructure, consequently affected populations are sometimes isolated and inaccessible due to the conflict. Additionally, victims of violence, especially women, have strong cultural disincentives to report sexual violence and little government, legal or material support to do so. This makes them susceptible to both continuing and additional forms of violence. Consequently, IDPs experience extreme vulnerabilities to structural violence because there is neither strong commitment nor structured efforts to address their plight.

With regard to gender violence, particularly VAW, literature on armed conflict and political violence situations (Giles and Hyndman 2004; McKay 1998; Meintjes, Pillay and Turshen 2002; Moser and Clark 2001; Pillay 2000; Turshen 2001) identifies the underlying causes of violence as unequal power relationships between men and women manifested in social practice and beliefs that promote male superiority and female inferiority; the social acceptance of VAW that is socially sanctioned as a form of discipline in peacetime and legitimises the use of violence during war and afterwards, and the construction of masculinity particularly through peer group pressure. The patriarchal structure of society enables men to use and abuse their power. Turshen (2001), in her analysis of the political economy of rape in Rwanda and Mozambique furthers the discourse in the systematic use of rape in civil war. War is used to strip women of their political and economic assets – reproductive and productive labour power and personal assets of property. Moser and Clark (2001) develop the concept of a gendered continuum of conflict and violence that encompasses social (inter-personal), political and economic violence. Critical to their analysis is the type of power that uses violence to gain or maintain power.

Additionally, Meintjes, Pillay and Turshen (2001) have addressed the gamut of violence in periods before, during and after the war. In all these periods, there is a relation of VAW to sexual control and the allocation of resources. This is especially so in the African tradition where most women do not have any access to resources in their own right. During war, rape becomes an important strategy of asset stripping by displacing populations from contested lands (Turshen 2001). In the aftermath of war, men use VAW and women's fear of violence to reinforce their hold on women compelling them to comply because men need to re-establish or preserve control over their wealth and resources, and above all women's productive and reproductive labour (Meintjes, Pillay and Turshen (2001). Indeed, these authors argue that the gender violence that women experience in war time increases when fighting dies down. This is supported by True (2012: 5) who points out that "post conflict and post-humanitarian crises and natural disaster processes have tended to deepen gender inequalities in economic and political participation, negatively affecting women's vulnerability to violence". This literature is critical to providing a framework for understanding violence in conflict and post-conflict situations by illuminating the structures of power that allow for violence against women to occur and continue.

In sum, the human rights framework in this chapter helps to contextualise the vulnerability of IDPs across the world and the practical and legal challenges of obtaining support from international actors due to their migration category (definition of IDPs). In addition, we have shown that even within an environment where international, regional and domestic human rights instruments exist, IDPs still remain susceptible to lack of basic security and exposed to other violations of their rights. Thus, the existence of normative frameworks has to be accompanied by a political will to implement them in order to safeguard the rights of IDPs. This suggestion allows us to investigate the structural conditions within Kenya that allowed the post-election conflicts leading to the encampment of men, women and children in Kenya, and to examine the continued human rights abuses in the camps. Importantly, we examine how the logic of the camps (to offer protection), originally developed as a technology for refugees, is not being deployed to manage IDPs. Ultimately, this has consequences for larger political structures of the Kenyan society and other countries with large IDP populations.

The following section discusses the methods we used for data collection in order to investigate these issues.

METHODS AND SOURCES OF DATA

Presenting the Voices of IDPs

As the title of the book suggests, we are concerned with presenting the voices of persons living in camps after the post-election violence in 2007-08. We aim to connect their daily experiences in the camps to larger social structural and institutional factors that have shaped these lives. Though our focus is on life in the camps, we note that these experiences are inflected by the election conflicts that took place post the 2007 presidential elections. Conditions of internally displaced persons (and refugees) are frequently told through stories and pictures that highlight their extreme vulnerability. These stories are sensitive enough and compel people to act in humanitarian ways. However, there is a need to move beyond individual-level stories to unravel the structural conditions that constantly shape the position of the IDPs in order to achieve this dual objective: (a) to highlight the voices of IDPs, and (b) to identify and analyse the structures that affect them. To achieve this, we gathered field data using two main methods: (1) semi-structured interviews and (2) ethnographic observations.

Semi-structured Interviews

The field interviews were conducted at two different periods. First, in 2008-09, Njiru was part of a team that conducted research on the situation of sexual and gender based violence in IDP camps following the post-election violence in 2007-08. The study was carried out in Nairobi and Rift Valley regions which experienced most of the violence. The assessment was part of the efforts of the Gender Based Violence sub cluster, an inter-agency sub cluster formed after the post-election violence to look into issues of gender violence in the camps, during and after the conflicts. The study was commissioned by the National Commission on Gender and Development to assist government and humanitarian agencies to respond to gender violence in the camps. The study utilised both a survey instrument and qualitative interviews. A total of 629 (400 female and 229 male) were randomly selected from original and transit camps. 249 (174 female and 75 male) IDPs participated in 28 focus group discussions. This research included key informant in-depth interviews with provincial administrators, law enforcers, humanitarian aid workers and camp leaders. We purposively selected 10 case studies from among the IDPs of people who had experiences gender violence. For this book, we use data from the qualitative interviews – focus group discussions, in-depth interviews and case studies – with women and men living in the camps, government workers and non-governmental organisations and agencies. This is because we aim to present *voices* of the internally displaced persons which tell their daily struggles in the camps.

Second, in the summer of 2012 Njiru conducted more in-depth interviews with nine women living in one of the camps in the Rift Valley region and further interviews with four government workers and five non-governmental organisations' staff involved in advocacy or service provision in the camps. It must be noted that since May 2008, after the post-election violence, the government of Kenya has been resettling IDPs, and therefore, many of the original and transition camps had closed down by the time of this second data collection phase. The interviews in the second phase were specifically geared towards examining the broader question of women's human rights violations in the camps.

In both study periods, the semi-structured interviews were conducted in the camps where participants felt most comfortable with either out in the field or in the participants' shelters. In order to gather information from a large number of people, the focus was on a varied age group, from eighteen to eighties. The aim of this broad age range was to gain as wide as possible an understanding of the daily lives of people living in the camps. Participants were asked about their back grounds; how they fled their homes during the violence; to describe their daily lives and conditions in the original formal camps they fled to; provision of services they receive in camps; describe daily lives and access to basic services in the current camps. From government and humanitarian staff, we were interested in their responses to the IDPs during and after the conflicts; their views on human rights violations, including gender violence. The interviews were carried out in three different languages – English (official language), Kiswahili (both official and national language) and Kikuyu (an ethnic language) – depending on each participant's level of education, ethnic background or language of choice. All interviews lasted between 1-2 hours. We transcribed the interviews and translated those that were in the local languages to English.

Ethnographic Observations

The semi-structured interview data was supplemented with ethnographic observations in the camps. Being part of the daily activities of some of the IDPs provided a better understanding of the structural impediments to accessing their rights. During both research periods, Njiru made observations of living conditions and infrastructure in the camps. In the period of the summer 2011 research, Njiru was able to spend more time in one camp participating in the daily activities of these women. She spent more time with women observing their chores in their tents or temporary houses. The participants welcomed her to their tents to show how they lived in congested, sometimes inhabitable conditions ignored by the government. She observed their activities outside the tents, for example, their interactions with other women and men in the camp. Sometimes she was able to observe them as they accessed various services from NGOs and government. For instance, she visited two government departments which were helping IDPs in livelihood reconstruction. Njiru also visited two NGOs that were running economic empowerment programmes for women including those displaced by the violence. In general, the observations were critical to understanding IDPs' lives, their interaction with various social institutions that address diverse needs in their lives, and how challenges with access to basic needs and services shaped their micro-level experiences within the camps, in their 'homes'.

Texts

In addition to the interviews and ethnographic observations, this book also relies on various IDP related texts – organisational and government reports, and policy documents on the election violence, during and after. Notably, there are numerous human rights organisational reports in Kenya that provide useful insights for this book. We made substantive references of the texts to examine human rights violations for men and women living in the camps.

OVERVIEW

Following this chapter on a broad overview of IDPs and human rights standards, we provide details about the socio-economic and political context in Kenya, including the nature and extent of violence. We focus on internally displaced persons to analyse the conditions in which they live in the camps. After that, we specifically emphasise on violence against women in the camps. In the last thematic chapter, we examine some of the response gaps to point out how they failed to achieve dignity for the IDPs and then provide a conclusion for our analysis.

The chapters, more specifically, are as follows:

Chapter 2. *Election Conflicts and Displacement*

In chapter two, we provide a background on Kenya and the Kenyan political scenario. We discuss the socio-economic and political conditions in Kenya that shape politically instigated ethnic conflicts. The Commission of Inquiry into the Post-Election Violence (CIPEV) in Kenya linked the conflicts to, among others, land and ethnic inequalities; high levels of unemployment among youth who easily join militias and ethnically organised gangs; failure of government to demobilise these gangs and militia groups; state violence particularly by state security agencies (CIPEV 2008); societal acceptance of violence, particularly violence against women (VAW); and failure to adequately address gender inequalities. We examine in more detail some of these structural conditions that allow politically instigated violence in Kenya and continue to shape human rights abuses in camps. We then discuss the nature and extent of displacements in Kenya since multi-party politics in 1991-2007 and focus on the post-election violence in 2007-08.

Chapter 3. *IDP Camps: The Situation*

The **third chapter** provides ethnographic details about living conditions in IDP camps. We, therefore, describe the physical setting of the camps. Then, through voices of IDPs, we examine infrastructure and sanitation facilities, availability of and accessibility to basic necessities such as food, water, health, education, security among others. We argue that it is important to highlight the physical setting and situation of basic services for IDPs living in camps because from a political perspective, camps are conceptualised as temporary spaces, yet, for the IDPs who have to live there for an indeterminate period of time, the camps are permanent places even in light of promises of resettlement by government. We also make links between the lives of IDPs and the structural circumstances discussed in chapter two. We argue that this structural violence exemplified by lack of basic services would indignify their lives.

Chapter 4. *Violence against Women in the Camps*

In **chapter four**, we specifically focus on violence against women. Women face far more consequences of violence during and after conflicts. They experience more serious forms of gender violence that may have long-term health consequences. We also show that women bear the arduous burden of taking care of their households and more often experience constant fear of further violence. In the chapter, we discuss various forms of violence experienced by women and young girls and explicate their relationship to the larger socio-structural forces. In doing so, we bring to the fore the continuum of violence before, during and after the conflicts and highlight the intricate linkages between private and public spheres of violence. To show this, we examine the ways in which violence within camps is integrally linked to policies, institutional arrangements and practices, including cultural norms and patriarchy that enable this violence and camp conditions, as discussed in chapters two and three.

Chapter 5. *Responding to IDPs Needs: The Twists, Turns and Rights*

In chapter five, we examine the interface between human rights standards and actual experiences of IDPs. We will provide a broad overview of some of the interventions for IDPs by both state and non-state actors. Our aim is not to describe or analyse all of the interventions but to use some cases to present a few of the structural challenges inherent in these interventions. We further show how these varying types and levels of intervention affect the lives of persons living in camps without wholly addressing their problems of shelter, food, health and vulnerability to violence.

Chapter 6. *Conclusion: Human Rights and Camp Life*

We discuss the implications of our study in the concluding **chapter six**. We emphasise how a human rights framework, that links the micro-level experiences of IDPs to the macro social and political structures in present day Kenya within a broader context of global economics and processes of colonialism and neo-colonialism, provides us with more nuanced knowledge of how structural violence leads to gross human rights violations, particularly for vulnerable populations. With specific reference to VAW, we highlight missing links between reporting violence and expectations of what will be and can be measured. In this endeavour, we attempt to answer the broader question of what it means to live in an IDP camp.

CHAPTER TWO

Kenya
Election Conflicts and Displacement

AN OUTLINE ON KENYA'S POLITICS PRE AND POST-INDEPENDENCE

Kenya lies on the east coast of Africa. The country has a population of about 40 Million people with more than 40 distinct ethnic groups. The name 'Kenya' was a colonial invention because the white settlers could not pronounce "Kirinyaga", the local name for Mt Kenya. Kenya was under British rule for close to 70 years, first as a British protectorate in 1895 and then officially as a colony since 1920. However, even before 1895, Britain's presence in Kenya was marked by dispossession and violence. British interest was in the Kenyan soil, particularly in the highlands (Kanyinga 2009). The colonial period was marked with resistance against the white settlers which was countered with excessive force by the colonial masters. Most of Kenya's modern history is marked by rebellions against the British. The last and most significant resistance movement was known as the Mau Mau rebellion that began in 1952. The outbreak of the Mau Mau paved the way for constitutional reforms and development in subsequent years.

In 1955, the colonial government gave in to the formation of political parties. In 1960, Kenya African National Union (KANU), a Kikuyu-Luo alliance, which advocated for a unitary government, was formed. In 1961, Kenya African Democratic Union (KADU) which advocated a quasi-federal government (Majimbo) was also formed. The first full general elections were held in May 1963 and KANU emerged the winner. On 1 June 1963, Kenya attained internal self-government. On 12 December of the same year, Kenya achieved independence with a complex Majimbo Constitution which conceded much autonomy to the regions. On the first anniversary of independence in 1964, Kenya became a Republic with Mzee Jomo Kenyatta as the President.

The independent Republic of Kenya was ruled as a *de facto* single-party state by the Kenya African National Union (KANU) from 1963 to 1978. Daniel arap Moi succeeded Kenyatta and ruled until 2002. Moi attempted to transform the *de facto* single-party status of Kenya into a *de jure* status during the 1980s, but came under pressure by external influences, particularly the US, and also massive internal resistance to single-party rule. He bowed to this pressure and restored a multi-party system in 1991. Moi was, however, elected twice after that, in 1992 and 1997 and ruled until 2002. His era was marked with numerous human rights abuses, including political assassinations, corruption and mismanagement of resources. Moi was constitutionally barred from running in the 2002 election, which was won by Mwai Kibaki. Though Mwai Kibaki was elected on a platform of ending corruption and reforms, the progress was slow and corruption continued to worsen inequalities in the country. This political scene largely shaped the 2007 post-election ethnic conflicts in which Mwai Kibaki was dubiously declared winner in an election marred with rigging.

Since Independence, Kenya has always been circumscribed by its failure to transcend its colonial past in its ability to reorganise its political-economic systems, including the bases for land ownership, which significantly enhance its stature and control over resource bases within the global political-economic system. Elected governments have failed to achieve adequate living conditions for most of the populace (Hornsby 2012). In fact, the gap between the poor and the rich has continued to widen. Additionally, Kenya's politics has been fraught with controversy. These reasons partly explain the roots behind post-election violence in 2007-08. The struggle for access to state resources and the employment of ethnicity for political patronage damaged Kenya's economy threatening the country's stability during the violence.

KENYA'S ECONOMIC SITUATION

Kenya is the largest economy in East Africa and its capital Nairobi is the regional commercial hub. Kenya's GDP stood at $33.62 billion in 2011 (World Bank 2011). Agriculture is the main economic driver of the country. Currently, tea, tourism and horticulture are the leading foreign exchange earners. Kenya also benefits significantly from remittances by Kenyans living abroad. After Independence, Kenya promoted rapid economic growth through public investment, encouragement of small-holder agricultural production, and incentives for private (often foreign) industrial investment. Gross domestic product (GDP) grew at an annual average of 6.6 per cent from 1963 to 1973 (Bunutu-Gomez 2011). Agricultural production grew significantly during the same period, stimulated by redistributing estates, diffusing new crop strains, and opening new areas to cultivation.

In 1980, Kenya became one of the first countries to sign a Structural Adjustment Loan with the World Bank. Over the next two decades, Kenya gradually replaced the import-substitution policies it had pursued since Independence with liberal economic strategy which included reduction of tariffs, slackening controls on imports, promoting export-promotion programmes, liberalisation of domestic markets and privatisation of state parastatals among others. The consequences of liberalisation were detrimental to the economy and the people of Kenya. The policies failed to deliver broad macro-economic success. During the 1980's and 1990's, after having experienced several years of strong growth during the early years of Independence, Kenya's economic performance began to fall. From 1991 to 1993, Kenya had its worst economic performance since Independence. Growth in GDP stagnated, and agricultural production shrank at an annual rate of 3.9 per cent. The economy grew by an annual average of only 1.5 per cent between 1997 and 2002, which was below the population growth estimated at 2.5 per cent per annum, leading to a decline in per capita incomes (Kenya Economic Centre 2013).

This poor economic performance is attributed to inappropriate agricultural, land and industrial policies compounded by poor international terms of trade and weaknesses in overall governance. Increased government intrusion into the private sector and import substitution strategy made the manufacturing sector uncompetitive. The policy environment, along with tight import restriction and foreign exchange controls, made the domestic environment for investment unattractive for both foreign and domestic investors. By 2002 when president Moi left office, Kenya's economic growth lagged at 1.1 per cent due to erratic rains, low investor confidence, meagre donor support, and political infighting up to the elections (Kuria 2007). A severe drought from 1999 to 2000 compounded Kenya's problems, from causing water and energy rationing to reducing agricultural output. The IMF, which had resumed loans in 2000 to help Kenya through the drought, again halted lending in 2001 when the government failed to institute several anticorruption measures.

During president Kibaki's first term, the government started an ambitious economic recovery and reform programme. In 2003, progress was made in rooting out corruption and encouraging donor support, and GDP rose slightly to 1.7 per cent though the government did not sustain efforts at eradicating corruption. Kenya's economic growth, however, began to recover in this period with real GDP growth registering 2.8 per cent in 2003, 4.3 per cent in 2004, 5.8 per cent in 2005, 6.1 per cent in 2006, and 7.0 per cent in 2007. However, the economic effects of the violence that broke out after the 27 December 2007 general election, compounded by drought and the global financial crises, brought growth down to less than 2 per cent in 2008. In 2009, there was modest improvement with 2.6 per cent growth. By the end of 2012, the country reported a growth of 4.7 per cent (US Department of State 2012).

The effects of the neo-liberal policies, corruption, drought, global financial crises have had dire consequences for the lives of the Kenya citizens. While the rich grow richer, the poor are getting poorer. There is also a burgeoning middle class as a result of the service sector industry and growth of the non-governmental organisations. About 60% of Kenya's population is currently living below a dollar a day. This implies that majority of Kenyans experience compounding effects of hunger, malnutrition, inaccessible basic health care and other essential needs and services. There is a high unemployment rate, particularly among the youth, many of who are educated. The post 2007 election violence is partly linked to the economic situation in the country.

THE 2007-08 POST-ELECTION CONFLICTS

In December 2007, Kenyans went to the polls heavily divided amongst two key presidential contestants; the incumbent president Mwai Kibaki and the leading opposition coalition led by Raila Odinga. The opposition political party hotly disputed the final vote count and result, but the Electoral Commission of Kenya announced the results late on 30 December 2007. Within hours of declaring Mwai Kibaki the winner of the disputed presidential poll, violence broke out in Nairobi, the Rift Valley, Coast, Western, and Nyanza provinces – regions where the opposition had overwhelming support. In the Rift Valley province, many Kikuyu families were evicted from their land holdings. Also evicted were members of the Kisii ethnic community, who were argued to have voted in support of the Kikuyu candidate, Mwai Kibaki. Kanyinga (2009) points out that the Kalenjin[5] evicted the Kikuyu, assumed control of areas on which the Kikuyu had settled, and in some cases gave them local Kalenjin names to erase the Kikuyu identity of the area.[6]

In the two months after the elections, political and social protests accompanied by violent attacks and the equally violent reaction by government security forces led to 'ethnic cleansing' particularly in the Rift Valley region. Ethnic polarisation, violence and neighbourhood struggles along ethnic lines led to the killing of more than 1,500 people and internal-displacement of an estimated 350,000-450,000 (International Commission of Jurists-Kenya and Kenya Human Rights commission 2012). The majority were from the Kikuyu ethnic group living in the Rift Valley, a predominantly Kalenjin region. Several reports and scholars (CREAW 2008; CIPEV 2008; Kanyinga 2009, UN Office of the High Commissioner for Human Rights 2008) have pointed out that the post-election violence took several dimensions.

First, it was spontaneous and took the form of protests in reaction to the perceived rigging of the election and the announcement of results after a flawed vote count. This first form of violence accompanied public demands for 'justice' and 'truth' about the election. The second form manifested in institutional violence in which security forces went out to oppositional strongholds to disperse by force those who were protesting. Third was the organised and coordinated violence: politicians and business people planned and signed up criminal gangs to execute violence. This form of violence had ethnic connotations; in the Rift Valley, it targeted the Kikuyu and the Kisii for expulsion from the region (Commission of Inquiry into the Post-Election Violence 2008). They had voted for the government and a Kikuyu candidate, yet they were settled in the Kalenjin's territorial sphere. The fourth pattern took the form of revenge attacks. These were organised especially by the Kikuyu to expel the Kalenjin, the Luo and the Luhya from their rented premises in parts of Nairobi, and from Naivasha and Nakuru in the eastern part of the Rift Valley province where the Kikuyu are numerically larger than other groups. Finally, there was a speedy spread of criminal violence that rapidly assumed a class dimension. Involved in all these forms of violence were groups of youth with financial support from their ethnic leaders and business people. Among the Kikuyu, for instance, Mungiki, an outlawed group which had sprouted from the first wave of political violence in 1991, was financed to undertake retaliatory attacks in Naivasha and Nakuru in the eastern part of the Rift Valley province. In the Rift Valley, Kalenjin warriors and several other militia groups also emerged to undertake attacks against the Kikuyu.

The December 2007 general election was the fourth that the country had conducted since the reintroduction of multi-party democracy in November 1991. Violent clashes had been reported during the 1992 and the 1997 elections, especially in the Rift Valley province and parts of the Coast province. However, the post 2007, election conflicts exceeded the prior ones in magnitude, intensity and extent in the country (CIPEV 2008). Unlike in the past where conflicts were mainly experienced in two regions, Rift Valley and Coast Valley province, this time six out of Kenya's eight provinces were involved in violent activities where the Rift Valley with a history of ethnic clashes was most affected. Notable is the fact that neither the 2002 general election nor the referendum on the proposed new Constitution in November 2005 – around which the governing coalition was deeply split and there were anti-Kikuyu feelings (Oloo 2010) – had triggered violent conflicts of a nature similar to what occurred during either the 1992 and 1997 or the 2007 elections.

International mediation by the African Union (AU) under the leadership of former UN Secretary General, Dr Kofi Annan, facilitated dialogue between the two political alliances and committed to a Kenya National Dialogue and

Reconciliation Process (KNDR), signed on 4 March 2008, to resolve the election crisis and to address long term solutions to election violence. This process developed four main agenda items: 1) Immediate action to stop the violence and restore fundamental rights and liberties (including disarmament and demobilisation of all armed groups and militia. Also, the Kenya Police Force and General Service Unit were required to act within the boundaries of the Constitution. 2) Address the humanitarian crisis, promote reconciliation, healing and restoration of calm. 3) Overcome political crisis. 4) Address long term issues and the root cause of the conflict, including constitutional, legal and institutional reforms (Wanyeki 2008). This national accord led to the establishment of a Commission of Inquiry into the Post-election Violence (CIPEV) and a Truth, Justice and Reconciliation Commission (TJRC). With respect to legal prosecution, four years after the post-election violence, the International Criminal Court (ICC) in January 2012 confirmed cases for four high level politicians and a senior government official for allegedly planning and funding the violence. These included the president and deputy president recently elected in March 2013. At the national level, the Kenyan police and local judicial system have failed to investigate crimes and to ensure justice for victims. The African Union Panel of Eminent African Personalities continues to monitor Kenya's implementation of the four agenda items.

The four-agenda KNDR agreement, however, came after months of painful deaths, loss of property, physical and psychological harm, and internal displacement of thousands of people across the country. For example, Nairobi Women's Hospital – Gender Violence Recovery Centre (GVRC) reported that during the violence, over 80 per cent (356) of the cases that they treated were related to sexual violence, nine per cent were of physical assault, seven per cent domestic violence related cases and four per cent were of indecent assault (CREAW 2008). It must be noted that this was a small figure representing only the people treated in that hospital. Many cases were treated in regional hospitals while others went undocumented. Today, six years after the post-election conflicts, many people continue to experience physical, sexual and a range of structural level violence.

EXPLAINING THE NATURE AND EXTENT OF ELECTION VIOLENCE AND DISPLACEMENTS IN KENYA

Violence and displacement have been part of Kenya's electoral process since multi-party politics in 1991. Despite pockets of electoral violence, Kenya was, however, viewed as an icon of political stability and economic prosperity in Africa until the December 2007 presidential election conflicts (Kanyinga 2009). The violence that followed this disputed elections thus called for the need to examine the processes that had gone wrong in Kenya. Nonetheless, as noted by Kanyinga (2009: 325) "researchers have tended to examine factors which are immediate rather than fundamental – the vote count as the trigger of the violence, for example, rather than on what predisposing conditions existed prior to the conflict" (See also Throup 2008).

There are several factors that contributed to the 2007 post-election violence. The Commission of Inquiry into the Post-Election Violence in Kenya was set up after the signing of the national accord (discussed above) to probe into the causes, nature and extent of the violence pointed out that these factors demonstrate "how and why violence has become a way of life in Kenya" (CIPEV: 2008 22). This normalisation of violence has deep roots in the systemic failure of government to address (ethnic) inequalities and ensure basic life conditions, failure to demobilise militia and other organised gangs, and lack of an effective oversight mechanism for reporting violence, among other factors.

In the next section, we discuss the land question and the rise of militia gangs in more detail.

The Land Question, Ethnic Inequalities and Political Violence

One of the most important roots of electoral violence in Kenya and, particularly the post 2007 election conflicts is inequalities in distribution and access to resources, especially land, given that about 79 per cent of the population lives in rural areas and relies on agriculture (CIPEV 2008). These inequalities are the basis of historical marginalisation of some ethnic groups – though sharp differences exist among members of the same group. Scholars of politics of land rights, ethnic inequalities, governance and development in Kenya agree that land is a key factor shaping electoral politics in Kenya (Harbeson 1973; Kanyinga 1998, 2009; Klopp 2001; Okoth-Ogendo 1981; Wily 2006). For example, Kanyinga (2009) argues, "the manner in which the question of access to and control of land rights in the former white highlands has been addressed throughout the post-colonial period constitutes a major factor responsible for the post 2007 election violence". He further asserts that the solution of the land question holds an important key to the future of Kenya as a nation state.

Scholars argue that the 2007 election violence has its deep roots in the way the colonial administration sought to 'redistribute' land and the processes and policies of post-independence land administration. The land question itself lies in the process that led to the establishment of the colonial settler economy (Sorrenson 1968; Okoth-Ogendo 1991). As pointed out by a leading land rights and political scientist scholar, Kanyinga (2009: 327):

> The first stage saw the alienation and acquisition of land by the protectorate. This was done before the colonial state was established. Second and soon afterwards was imposition of English property law, which ratified the appropriation of land already alienated and acquired. It also provided a justification for further expropriation. The third step was reform of land tenure, where customary rights to land were restructured through individualisation

> or privatisation of land. Fourth was alienation of land for the purpose of establishing a colonial settler economy. This last step had more consequences for the country's land question. Land expropriated included part of the Ukambani region in the Eastern province, Central Kenya, and the Rift Valley whose land had the greatest potential. The land was chosen because the white settlers had to be attracted to the area by the confidence that it would be of permanent use (Sorrenson 1968).

Following this was introduction of laws that facilitated land expropriation and alienation such as the Crown Lands Ordinance of 1915 which introduced a dual system of land administration and political governance. It bifurcated land into land for Africans or ('native reserves') and 'scheduled land' (or white highlands) for European settlement. This took away all the land rights of the Africans and vested those rights in the crown (Okoth-Ogendo 1991). Introduction of the tax system saw migration of Kenyans (especially the Kikuyu) to the white highlands in search of wage labour on settler farms (Brett 1973; Berman 1990). What is significant for ethnicisation of the Kenyan society was that each of the land units in the natives' land was reserved for a particular ethnic group (Kanyinga 2009). Thus, in Kenya, establishing a settler economy involved restructuring of mechanisms of control of land and access to land rights. New land reforms and the introduction of individualisation, first among the Kikuyu of Central Kenya, added to the evolving problem of land rights. These people migrated to the white highlands in search of employment, adding to the number of squatters already settled there. How the problem of land rights was settled at Independence contributed significantly to the shaping of ethnic dimensions of the land question.

Scholars note that in post-independence Kenya, the resettlement efforts that followed immediately after Independence created a fertile ground for fomenting ethnic dissensions and for future ethnic conflicts (Kanyinga 2009).

The land reform programme, starting from early 1960s, took place alongside discussions about political independence. This meant that each form of negotiation, for land and political independence, informed the other. Therefore, ethnicity inevitably influenced political negotiations and dealing with land issues stirred up ethnic identities which in turn fed into national politics. As noted by Kanyinga (2009: 332), "various groups sought to separate or to be together with others depending on the threats they thought other groups posed to their land".

The solution to landlessness thus resulted in ethnicity becoming an important factor in the land problem and also in national politics. For example, communities in the Rift Valley province resented efforts at settlement schemes and the land purchase programme because they tended to benefit the Kikuyu ethnic group in an area that the Kalenjin considered to be their own. This contributed to ethno-political conflicts from the 1960s. Kanyinga points out that the Kikuyus were able to organise and buy land in the Kalenjin-Rift Valley region because they had the support of Kikuyu and allied members (Meru) in government. Researchers have argued that the government's attempt to address the land question in the 1960s via settlement schemes and the land purchase programme sought to ensure economic stability of the new administration by eradicating the only possible source of political unrest – the Kikuyu landless in Rift Valley. This produced new social-political contradictions, deepened ethnic animosity and later became the basis for inter-ethnic conflicts (Kanyinga 2009).

In the 1970s and 1980s, although the settlement schemes were contested, there were no organised forms of violence to evict the Kikuyu from the Rift Valley. Government thwarted attempts by the radical Kalenjin politicians to evict the Kikuyu. Nonetheless, in 1991 the re-introduction of multiparty politics saw a resurgence of political violence beginning in the Rift Valley. Leaders from some of the numerically large communities, the Kikuyu and the Luo, whom Moi had marginalised from power, demanded multi-party democracy. Moi and KANU responded violently and the Kalenjin politicians allied with Moi and KANU used 'land' as the symbol to mobilise ethnic support in the Rift Valley. They argued that those in the political opposition demanding multiparty democracy, and the Kikuyu, in particular, had secured land in the Rift Valley meant for the Kalenjin and the Maasai who had historical territorial claims to the area. From then on, political campaigns were built on the land question and the need to reintroduce a majimbo (semi-federal) system of government so that groups in the Rift Valley could take control of their lands (Kanyinga 2009). This form of political exclusion sought to eliminate those opposed to Moi – the Kikuyu who were in the opposition – by evicting them from land they had occupied in the settlement schemes or bought through the land purchase programme. A specific example of heightened ethnic animosity was in October 1991 when majimboists in KANU invaded farms in the Rift Valley to evict non-Kalenjin through a campaign against 'foreigners or settlers' (National Council of Churches of Kenya 1992; Parliamentary Select Committee Report 1992). A repeat of the same occurred close to the 1997 general election. Once more, the Kalenjin elites in KANU mobilised around the land question. They continually pointed out that the Kikuyu had not only acquired what was Kalenjin land but also that the Kikuyu were rapidly dominating the local economy at the expense of Kalenjin. Because of these discourses of domination, violence related to land and targeting specifically the Kikuyu in the Rift Valley continued to follow election cycles. The Kikuyu peasants became the main victims of these waves of evictions (Kanyinga 2009). Involved in these cycles of violence were groups of Kalenjin youth organised under the name of Kalenjin warriors and guided by both senior and local politicians who also financed their operations (Commission of Inquiry into the Post-Election Violence 2008). However, the 2002 election and the referendum of 2005 did not witness these forms of violence. There were no threats against the Kikuyu in the Rift Valley.[7] On 30 December 2007, immediately after the presidential results were announced, extreme violence broke out in Kenya when gangs of violent youth attacked and evicted people from their homes and land, once again bringing into fore the role of politically motivated militia groups in the uneasy nexus of ethnicity, land and politics in Kenya.

MILITIA AND ORGANISED GANGS IN KENYA

Several reports on the post-election violence have established in unequivocal terms that vital links existed between militia gangs and violence that erupted immediately after the announcement of the 2007 election results. The emergence of militias and violent gangs, like the ethnic question, is linked to the unequal redistribution of national resources – especially land, marginalisation of some communities, and the ever rising income disparities. This is as a result of post-independent state policies that have resulted in horizontal or systemic inequalities between groups (Oloo 2010). As Oloo opines, these inequalities have generated powerful grievances which leaders exploit to mobilise people to protest by calling on cultural cards (a common history, language or religion), thus exploiting the masses at group level. Marginalisation and inequalities in the distribution of power and resources have resulted in various ethnic groups creating political parties headed by one of their own with the hope that if they capture power, they will benefit from access to state resources. Electoral politics in Kenya thus consists of highly cohesive bloc-voting ethnic groups. Kenyans generally vote for the same party as their ethnic kin, and particularly so if a contending party has a representative from their own community as a presidential candidate. Political parties are usually formed on the basis of ethnicity and personal ties rather than by ideological commitment. Even where coalitions have been formed, they have been coalitions of ethnic groups rather than coalitions of parties that share the same ideological commitment. Formation of ethnic political parties has often gone hand in hand with the formation of militant groups that claim to safeguard the interests of their specific communities (Oloo 2010).

According to Oloo, the history of militias in Kenya can be traced to the war waged by the Mau Mau against the British rule in the 1950s. Among the issues that led to the Mau Mau revolt were land scarcity, forced labour and meagre wages. In post-independence Kenya, the phenomenon of the militia group has its roots in the creation of a youth wing by the former ruling party, KANU. The KANU regime first used its youth wing to harass the first opposition party, KADU, which existed for only one year after independence. Youth-wingers were, however, used more forcefully after a split in KANU saw the formation of the Kenya People's Union (KPU). Since then, all elections during the one party era witnessed violence meted out by youth-wingers, with prominent politicians hiring the youth to disrupt their opponents' rallies. As pointed out by Oloo, the KANU youth wingers gave birth to the rise of criminal militias even after the country returned to multi-party politics. The youth wingers were important in the formation and rise of the Mungiki (meaning multitude in the Kikuyu language) in the post 1992 election period. It is a banned organisation that favours a return to indigenous African traditions. The Mungiki, for example, attacked groups that had assailed and displaced Kikuyus settled in the Rift Valley region.

The multi-party period, especially the Moi era, saw the formation and metamorphosis of these groups into criminal gangs and militias. They used force to intimidate voters to vote for KANU, the party led by Moi. Oloo points out that in 1992, these groups were operating mainly from Moi's political base in the Rift Valley, where the *Kalenjin Warriors* and *Maasai Morans* attacked rival ethnic groups. In 1997, these groups were being trained and armed in the Coast province (Kaya Bombo) and recruited, trained and organised in the Shimba hills, Kaya Waa and the Similani caves in the Kwale district, at the instigation of prominent politicians and with the support of the government and the military. They were then deployed to stir up ethnic violence in the run-up to the 1997 elections at the Coast.

As opposition groups became increasingly vulnerable to state-sponsored militias, they resorted to creating their own armed forces to provide protection for opposition parties during election campaigns. Some of the opposition-sponsored criminal gangs and militias were the *Jeshi la Embakasi, Baghdad Boys* and *Amachuma*. As noted by Oloo (2010), the result of this has been a growth of self-styled militias, vigilante groups and organised criminal gangs in both urban and rural areas that have sprouted in almost every part of the country, posing an increasing challenge to a poorly trained and ill-equipped police force. The most notorious of these gangs were the *Mungiki* (Nairobi/Rift Valley/Central), SLDF (Mount Elgon), *Kaya Bombo Youth* (Mombasa/Kwale), *Sungu Sungu, Chinkororo* and *Amachuma* (Kisii/Nyamira/Gucha/Transmara) and *Taliban, Jeshi la Mzee* and *Jeshi la Embakasi* (Nairobi). In most times, these violent groups share a common ethnic background just like the ethnic political parties with whom they are associated. These gangs often operate on the basis of local political concerns and forms of mobilisation, which may include language, faith and traditional practices. For example, *Mungiki* is associated with the Kikuyu, the *Baghdad Boys* and *Taliban* with the Luo, the *Chinkororo* with the Kisii, the *Angola-Musumbiji* with the Luhya, the *Kalenjin Warriors* with the Kalenjin, the *Maasai Morans* with the Maasai, the *Kaya Bombo* with the Coastal tribes, and the SLDF with the Sabaot.

The emergence of gangs is also linked to government's concern with amassing and maintaining political power in the 1990s rather than maintaining infrastructure and service provision. As service provision declined and insecurity increased, gangs stepped in to 'provide' some of these services at a fee, particularly in the informal settlements in urban areas, thus making them extremely powerful. Therefore, the government's inability to meet the basic welfare of its people has immensely contributed to the proliferation of gangs who take charge of fraudulent service provision and force people to pay for these services such as illegal power and water connection to the informal settlements.

Additionally, most of these gangs are composed of marginalised youth in society, especially the urban and rural poor. Kenya has a growing population of poor, unemployed youth, both educated and uneducated. The CIPEV (2008) reports that this population includes adult street children – children who grew up living in the streets – many of who are the products of past displacements by ethnic violence as well. This population, in search of a livelihood, easily agrees to join militias and ethnically organised gangs. Politicians have used these gangs to create hatred and violence against other individuals and communities particularly during the electoral period. Over the years, the gangs have come to wield an immense amount of power in the country.

CONCLUSION

In this chapter we presented the macro-structures that have shaped Kenya's political and economic history. In particular, the processes of colonialism and their aftermath in post-independence Kenya and the global neo-liberal economic policies continue to play a significant role in the social, economic, cultural and political environment in Kenya. For example, the outcome of the land redistribution policy of the 1960s appears to have shaped the December 2007 presidential election disputes. Both the procedure by which land settlement schemes were established and the skewed bias in favour of certain groups are responsible for the recurrence of electoral violence. Furthermore, land becomes the symbol for organisation of ethnic identities which are mobilised for political purposes including conflict. As Kanyinga (2009) has pointed out, there is a clear link between land, territory and politics.

Additionally, the proliferation of militia gangs has roots in the colonial resistance movements in pre-independence Kenya. In the post-independence period, the gangs have played a key role to safeguard the interests of politician and ethnic groups. We have noted that these gangs usually constitute of the rural and urban poor, including educated persons who cannot find meaningful work due to the high unemployment levels in the country. Moreover, their proliferation has been enhanced by successive governments failure to de-mobilise them because of their relationship to the political class, their control over vast expanses in the country, and because state security agents have been victims of the gangs or protected them (CIPEV 2008). Their presence and endurance have thus become a security threat to the nation. As scholars have shown, these gangs played a key role in the 2007-08 post-election violence and displacements of thousands of Kenyans. These structural factors, among others, contributed to the hundreds of thousands of displacements, and physical, sexual and psychological harm and other forms of gender violence. These factors continued to shape the lives of internally displaced persons in the camps to which they fled after the evictions. With this background in mind, we now turn to describe and discuss the experiences of IDPs in the camps in the following chapter.

CHAPTER THREE

IDP Camps and the Living Conditions

I am a 30-year-old married male with one child. I came to the Narok camp from Enosupukia. When we came to the camp, many of us were physically hurt. NGOs, government and well-wishers helped us with food and clothes and sometimes, we men, gave the only shirt we had to the women to cover their children at night. But things have changed now. The government has come in and lied to us that we will get money tomorrow. It has come to divide the people. We have very many needs and concerns in the camp. I have suffered a lot. Prior to the clashes, I was able to provide for my family but now I cannot. I am grateful that I have clothes which came from well-wishers but we have no food and we also lack medicine when we get sick. Men sometimes go to look for jobs in town but may lack. (Male, 30 years)

We request the government to take us back home. During the early days there was food but now there is none. People go hungry even for three days. Nobody attends to old people. Nowadays we keep asking if we are human beings or animals on earth. Those with money eat, those without go with no food for days. (Female, 41 years)

We have many problems here; food and shelter are major problems. Look at the conditions of the tents. When it is hot they are extremely hot and when it is cold they get extremely cold. Also, since we came here my husband has been admitted to hospital twice because of stress. We had a farm and he was running a business and these were reduced to nothing. (Married female, 46 years)

These quotations highlight the living conditions in the camps which are the focal issues of this chapter. While the last chapters indicated the circumstances that led to internal displacement, in this chapter and the next, we focus on life in camps. In this chapter, we foreground voices of IDPs as we provide ethnographic details that describe their experiences with provision of basic services in the camps such as housing and sanitation, food and water, health and education. These structural conditions lie at the heart of IDPs vulnerabilities to violence and their ability to move beyond violence-prone lives.

As we noted in the first chapter, although there is no specific international legal framework to address the needs of IDPs, international human rights law has imposed obligations on states to address all citizens' needs, including those who have been displaced for various reasons. For example, Article 1 of the African Charter on Human and Peoples' Rights (ACHPR) stipulates that member states of the OAU party to the Charter "shall recognise the rights, duties and freedoms enshrined in this Charter and shall undertake to adopt legislative or other measures to give effect to them". Similarly, Article 2 (1) of the ICSECR provides each party to the Covenant "undertakes to take steps, individually and through international assistance and co-operation, especially economic and technical, to the maximum of its available resources, with a view to achieving progressively the full realisation of the rights recognised in the present Covenant by all appropriate means, including particularly the adoption of legislative measures". Domestically, the Kenyan Constitution guarantees human rights. Various articles of these documents stipulate that states recognise the right of everyone to, among others, food, highest attainable standard of physical and mental health, education, clothing and housing, right to work, security, and the continuous improvement of living conditions. Therefore, the state has the responsibility to uphold and ensure the human rights of IDPs as with any other citizen. We, however, do not propose to hold the state solely responsible for the protection of its citizens' rights. As Ertürk (2006) has pointed out, there is also need to recognise how state authority and power are reconfigured and challenged by non-state actors thus holding them responsible too.

We further note from the onset of this chapter that from a socio-political point of view, camps are temporary and thus seen as makeshift measures of service provision. Yet, for the men and women living in the camps, the need for basic goods and services acquires a certain degree of permanency, despite resettlement promises by the government. Therefore, even as camps became more permanent dwelling places for IDPs who continued to live there every day, the Kenya government did not prioritise the fulfilment of basic needs because they viewed them as temporary. We start with a brief overview of the types of camps that emerged after the election conflicts.

TYPES OF CAMPS

Immediately following the declaration of Mwai Kibaki as the winner of the presidential election on Sunday, 30 December 2007, violence broke out in various parts of the country. Kibaki was sworn in, in a hurriedly prepared ceremony in State house in Nairobi, almost an hour after the poll-announcement as violence erupted. According to reports (CIPEV 2008), tension built up during the election campaigns and went on as the vote counting process was in progress. The violence was initially targeted at Kibaki supporters. For example, in the Rift Valley, there were warning signs for the *madoadoa* (Swahili word meaning spots and used especially to refer to Kikuyus who have settled in the Rift Valley region) to return to their original community from which they migrated should the vote count be in favour of the incumbent president, Mwai kibaki, a Kikuyu (CIPEV 2008). When violence broke out, 'foreign' ethnic groups began to flee or were forcefully evicted from their homes by their host communities. The conflicts consequently led to the emergence of various types of camps typifying government and other humanitarian responses to the crisis.

Formal/Original Camps

As the violence erupted, people began to flee their homes to public spaces such as, schools, church compounds, police stations, chief's camps, prison compounds and agricultural show grounds. The initial response by the government was to evacuate people from places in their local hostile communities they had fled to, where there were fears of further attacks, and take them to secure places for protection. The initial places formed what the government called original or formal camps. These camps were overall managed by the government of Kenya, Kenya Red Cross and UNHCR through the UN-led cluster approach (discussed further in chapter five) for responding to humanitarian crises. The cluster approach brought together UN and non-UN agencies, NGOs and civil society organisations to ensure a coordinated response.

Transit Camps

The transit camps originated from the government's resettlement programme. After the signing of the Kenya National Dialogue and Reconciliation (KNDR) accord mediated by the African Union (AU) under the leadership of the former UN Secretary General, Dr Kofi Annan, the government committed to ensure quick and fair resettlement or return of those who were displaced during the violence.[8] In May 2008, the government launched "Operation Rudi Nyumbani" (ORN-Operation Return Home), a programme aimed at resettling IDPs.

They offered 25,000 Kenyan shillings (approximately USD 290) to the IDPs whose houses were burnt or destroyed and 10,000 Kenya shillings (approximately USD 118) to those whose homes were looted. The programme had several components: increasing physical security (for example, they constructed 30 new police posts where the IDPs were returning), rehabilitate key services (rebuild destroyed schools, clinics, markets and bridges), provide IDPs with assistance for the first three months of return (food, seeds, fertiliser and farm tools to restart livelihoods) and engage in peace and reconciliation activities with the host communities to end inter-ethnic tensions (Kamungi 2011).

Many human rights organisations, particularly the Kenya Human Rights Commission and the IDP Network have noted that this exercise evidenced force, threats and lies to the IDPs in order to close the camps (KHRC 2009). For instance, during the 2008 data collection exercise in the Rift Valley, our research team found the *General Service Unit* (GSU), a paramilitary wing of the Kenyan Military and Kenyan Police, evicting IDPs from one of the camps and we were, therefore, not able to interview them. The *GSU* put them in military trucks and drove them off to their pre-displacement homes. Furthermore, as has been reported by several human rights organisations, to put pressure on IDPs to leave camps, the government discontinued essential services such as water and barred humanitarian and other NGOs and well-wishers from providing assistance to the IDPs.[9]

What followed this operation was that majority of the IDPs could not return to their homes because they found that the host community was still hostile and did not allow them back to their houses and farms despite talks of reconciliation meetings. In fact, Kanyinga (2009) has pointed out that some IDPs found that their host communities had changed names of the areas where the IDPs had lived before displacement, implying that they did not want them back at all. These IDPs consequently set up other camps close to their farms. This way, they were able to access their farms in the day and return to the camps in the evening. They could not sleep in their former homes due to threats and fear of attack. These camps were referred to as the transit or satellite camps. The government seemed to have been more concerned with fulfilling the requirements in agenda two of the KNDR – instituting immediate measures to address the humanitarian crisis, and promote healing and reconciliation – than ensuring a dignified return of the IDPs to their homes or to other safe lands. There was need for the government to also show the international community that they had dealt with the crisis. In the long run, one would argue that the ORN was an expensive exercise, because the IDPs in transit camps continued to require assistance from government in the following years.

Self-help Camps

The third type of camps has been categorised as the self-help camps. When government offered money for IDPs to return to their homes, there were IDPs who had fear of returning to their farms anticipating further attacks. Using the little money offered by the government, they registered self-help groups that enabled them to collectively purchase land because they would not have been able to do so in their individual efforts. They moved with their tents to the purchased land. Other IDPs moved to land donated by well-wishers. In both cases, the land was in remote and underserviced areas and the IDPs continued to rely on organisations and well-wishers for housing and other basic services as the government had greatly reduced support to IDPs. In spite of this typology of camps, living conditions in the camps were similar, as we describe and discuss here below.

PHYSICAL SETTING OF THE CAMPS

SHELTER, WATER AND SANITATION

The people fleeing violence were mainly sheltered in tented camps. The primary goal of the camps was to ensure that they were isolated and protected from their attackers. When violence broke out and forceful evictions began, people initially fled to the nearest public spaces in their communities such as church compounds, police stations, and chiefs' camps. In these places, they slept on cold floors and had nothing to cover themselves with for days. The government then evacuated them from the communities where they were susceptible to further attacks and transported them to the original camps that could accommodate more people and where they would be better managed and protected. The government and humanitarian relief agencies, Faith Based Organisations (FBOs), Community Based Organisations (CBOs) and other well-wishers responded to their plight with urgency by providing more urgent items like tents and blankets. At the same time, the number of IDPs continued to rise even as the government and humanitarian agencies sought ways to deal with the overwhelming crisis that had caught them unprepared.

The rising number of IDPs was a challenge to government and relief agencies. Depending on the infrastructure available where the IDPs were sheltered, they either slept in halls or in tents. All the IDPs interviewed in two phases of this study highlighted that the physical conditions in the camps were challenging. They complained of sleeping on cold floors, torn tents, thin mattresses, lack of blankets and lack of privacy. They also decried congestion. Families shared a single tent regardless of the number of children. Additionally, the tents had no room partitions. Both parents and their children slept in the same room. The following excerpts exemplify the conditions in the camps.

> I am a young girl aged 19 years old. I fled from Kibera slum in January immediately after the violence broke out. Life is hard, it is not the life I used to live. Now I have been forced to move in with my mother and yet I was living alone before. I am not free because I share a tent with my parents. I feel very uncomfortable. We have old men in the camp and we share tents and hall with them.

> You know we are used to sleeping naked at night, we throw our blankets away. But these old men now see our bodies and we feel so embarrassed. Life is just so hard. (Maureen, female, 19 years)

> My husband beat me up because I refused to have sex with him. He came back home at night drunk and was loudly demanding for sex in presence of the children. Our tents are very small and we have three children but he still wants me to have sex. Some couples quarrel until they throw each other out of their tents like my neighbours did. (Jessica, female, 45 years)

The quotations above regarding the physical condition of the camps raised several concerns for the IDPs. Maureen complained of the sleeping arrangements and lack of physical privacy in the camps. She feared exposing her body to older men while sleeping, particularly her father. She reminded us that it was against her culture for her father to see her naked body, even though she would be sleeping and unaware that her father might see her nakedness. This made her feel very embarrassed and unable to face her father. On the other hand, Jessica talked about compounding problems that sleeping in a tent brings for her. Her husband physically beat her up because she refused to have sex with him in presence of her children. But how could she have sex while her three children were sleeping right next to her? She asked. In addition, she noted that she was not the only one experiencing violence; other married couples also "fight until they throw each other out of their tents". Therefore, congestion and poor sleeping arrangements in the camps resulted in either feelings of embarrassment, tension and conflicts in the families and loss of physical integrity. Congestion was also critically linked to poor sanitation and health concerns (that we discuss below) in the camps.

Camps lacked proper and adequate sanitation facilities. In addition, there was an inadequate water supply that could improve sanitation in the camps. The common pit latrines and bathrooms were not enough given the population of IDPs. For example, at the time of this research, many of the pit latrines were full of human waste but they were not covered. This predisposed IDPs, both adults and children, to diseases. According to a senior government official, the pit latrines were quickly filling up and it would take a lot of space to dig more, yet there was no space. Mobile toilets were better solutions but even these were filthy. Water shortage and improper disposal of domestic waste compounded sanitation problems for the IDPs. A senior officer pointed out that government was aware of the risks posed by poor sanitation but defended it arguing that the authorities were overwhelmed with the large numbers of IDPs. There were inadequate resources to deal with sanitation that would promote the health of IDPs:

> Health conditions. Okay, those are deplorable because of the numbers. Number two, most of the camps didn't have water. Number three, okay, they were digging pit latrines but they were filling at such a high rate and therefore, they would dig, they fill and therefore, you know areas which had pit latrines were becoming larger and larger.

Since there was not enough space to put up more latrines or proper mechanisms for disposing off the human waste, the areas around the latrines were inhabitable. So deplorable was the situation in some camps that some IDPs reported that they had stopped using the facilities and went to find toilets outside the camps or helped themselves in the bush, depending on the location of the camp. In addition to the scarce toilet facilities, there were insufficient bathrooms or places to take showers in the camps. Both the bathrooms and toilets were shared by all people – men, women and children of all ages. Yet, many of these facilities did not have lockable doors and were not properly lit. These two issues compromised privacy and security, particularly in the night for the women and girls. In the camps we visited, privacy was a major concern. Women such as Miriam below felt that these facilities created risks of sexual violence:

> Here we have one bathroom for both men and women. The bathroom is torn and people would see you when you are showering. When the men go to the bathroom, they find our panties there and throw them away, yet you only have that one. Also, there was a case the other day of a girl who was sexually assaulted as she went to the toilet in the evening. Now, when we want to use the bathrooms, we have to go in groups. (Miriam, female, 22 years)

Assessments by humanitarian agencies and other organisations (under the United Nations Protection Cluster) on various risk factors in the camps led to building separate toilets for men and women, installation of lighting and more organised sleeping quarters, even though these still remained squalid.

The issue of poor infrastructure, congestion and sanitation facilities was replicated in the transit and self-help camps. As noted earlier, when the government rolled out the resettlement programme in May 2008, the expectation was that IDPs would be able to return to their pre-displacement homes or to rebuild their lives. On the contrary, as it turned out, many IDPs either experienced or feared further attacks by the host community and were, therefore, not able to go back home. Many retuning IDPs who put up transit camps or those in the self-help camps found themselves in a similar cycle of poor housing, water shortages and inadequate sanitation. Yet, there was even less support from the government in terms of providing basic services. For example, in one of the self-help camps we visited, the latrines were so filthy that the women in the camp begged the researcher not to go near them when she tried to find out their condition. The IDPs in transit and self-help camps continued to rely on support. For instance, organisations such as Habitat for Humanity helped to construct houses for some of the IDPs who had purchased their own land.

FOOD AND NUTRITION

One of the issues that receives the greatest coverage for encamped persons is food. The right to food is inviolable. However, it must be noted that the violation of the right to food is not a problem only for the internally displaced persons in Kenya. In general, more than half of the country's 40 million population lives below the poverty line, on less than one US dollar a day (UNICEF 2013). The United Nations Development Programme (UNDP 2013) ranked Kenya at 145 out of 186 countries, in the level of low human development. Inequalities are wide with the top 10 per cent of Kenyans earning 44 per cent of the national income, while the bottom 10 per cent earns less than one per cent. It is, however, ironic that poverty (at a rate of 48 per cent), or the inability to meet daily nutritional requirements is a big issue in a country that has one of the best developed economies in Eastern Africa. Approximately 80 per cent of the population lives in the rural areas and mainly depends on smallholder subsistence agriculture, which produces about 75 per cent of total agricultural output. Nonetheless, the violation of the right to food, that makes countries such as Kenya dependent on relief food, particularly in times of crisis such as the post-election violence, has to be seen in the wider context of the global social, economic and political relations and inequalities in the production and marketing of food. These inequalities coupled with internal country factors such as the gross income inequalities in the population and mismanagement of resources affect access to food.

Internally displaced persons living in camps experienced immense challenges with respect to availability of adequate food. Majority of the post-election violence survivors were displaced from their farms and businesses resulting in the loss of economic livelihoods. In the camps, they faced challenges of inadequate food and nutrition. Interviews with IDPs in all the camps revealed that their main concern was food, as the story of John informs us:

> We have a problem with food here. When we came to the showground, we had to queue for food. Sometimes the food would get finished before some people had the chance to eat. Later when we were grouped into families and given tents, we were also given cooking utensils. Red Cross and government then started distributing food – mainly maize and beans per family. It was very little for the families to survive on. We don't get enough food. We are given maize only so we are forced to sell the maize in order to buy soap and milk for our children. (Ben, Married Male, 27 years)

Ben, a father of two young children, was evicted from his farm. He talked about his experiences and challenges with food in an Eldoret camp. When they fled to the camp, they had to queue for food. The food was not enough and sometimes those on the queue did not get food and went hungry. According to Ben, there would be a lot of pushing on the queue. This means that only those who had the energy to push and shove were lucky to get food. The providers did not consider that some people did not have the capacity to queue, such as the sick, elderly, disabled and some women. In the same camp, the media reported on the problems of disabled persons. A man aged 56 years, who was disabled and on a wheelchair had observed, "I cannot fight and push over food when the Kenya Red Cross Society serves it. I depend on well-wishers or go without food for days" (East African Standard, 31 March 2008). Later, families were given their own cooking utensils so that they would be given food to cook for themselves. The food rations, according to Ben, were inadequate and consisted of maize and beans. As a family with young children, Ben says that sometimes parents sold their food rations, either to other IDPs or to the residents outside the camps in order to buy milk for the children. This was before the government started providing milk powder for families with children. Not only was there concern for young children, but IDPs in general had other needs such as bathing soap, sanitary towels, and they sold their food to meet these extra family needs. As Ben sums up his story, he says "the going is tough at the camp".

John's experience as a young father dealing with the crisis of food in the camp resonated with many other similar IDPs' experiences. In addition, women talked of their unique disadvantages in accessing food and their experiences with husbands who sold food in order to buy alcohol thus exacerbating the problem of hunger in the camps. As Alice recollects:

> There is a lot of violence during the distribution of food. In fact, you can be killed (sic) by the men. Men here don't provide food for the women but they fight and beat their wives for the food so that they can sell and get Ksh 20 but a woman with a baby misses the food because she is unable to fight the energetic husband. When a woman finds work she feeds the entire family, men use the money to buy cheap beer. Women really help because the food that we are given is not enough. You may be told that you have been given a kilogram (of food ration) only to discover that it is a half or a quarter. When men come back in the evening and find that the woman has brought back some money, they are grateful that she brought something home regardless of the means she used, whether moral or immoral.

Alice points to several issues linked to inadequate food provision in the camp and which from a rights perspective violates several rights. As with John and the media report, Alice talks about women as a category of persons who sometimes suffered hunger because they were sometimes pushed from the queue by the more energetic men. At other times, men sold the food rations to buy alcohol, yet it was the burden of the women to ensure that their families were fed. Women, therefore, took on various jobs outside the camps in the towns or farms in order to provide for their families. At other times, as Alice suggests, they took on "immoral" jobs, implying sex work. Interestingly, she says that the husbands did not mind the means women used to obtain food. However, conversations with other women revealed that suspicions of extra marital relations or sex work caused intense conflicts in the families and there were many separations between partners in the camps.

Another major problem with the supply of relief food to the IDPs was the government bureaucracy and claims of looting or favouritism in the distribution of the limited food. In order to effectively manage IDP camps, IDPs appointed leaders who worked with government and other humanitarian organisations to manage affairs of the camps. One of their duties was to ensure that every person in the camp was supplied with food. They also kept a register of IDPs which they used during food distribution to ensure that only genuine IDPs living in the camp received food. Despite the existence of this leadership structure, there were numerous cases of malpractices in food distribution where some leaders were accused of favouritism and stealing food, as observed by the following IDPs:

> Yes, we have leaders but they are divided into two. There are those who are accountable to IDPs and leaders accountable to a clique of people. When food is brought they favour them. (Single female, 27 years)

> Our leaders were very good at the beginning, we loved them. But now something has gone wrong. I do not know exactly whether it is greed or lust. They have forgotten that we were only seeking shelter then return to where we came from. We no longer trust our leaders to be fair

> in distributing supplies. Whenever they get aid, they always give us less. (Married male, 43 years)

> Some leaders are corrupt, they hide relief food. Like yesterday they were given milk powder to distribute but they did not. When people in the camp got to know, there was chaos. (Single male, 32 years)

The claims of looting food have to be seen in light of inadequate food supplies by government which then forces people engaged in distribution to involve in malpractices. As noted above, some IDPs sold their food in order to meet other family needs that the government did not meet. It is not, therefore, surprising that camp leaders, who were part of the IDPs, would sell the food in order to meet other non-food needs.

In addition, when government began the ORN resettlement programme in May 2008, they reduced food supplies as part of the scheme to 'facilitate' resettlement. In fact, the researchers were told that some men had used the money offered for resettlement for alcohol consumption since it was inadequate to rebuild their lives. Therefore, many of the IDPs who prolonged their stay in the formal camps, after receiving the government offer, remained there without outside help. As observed by the following participants, food became even scarcer during the resettlement period:

> During the early days there was food but now there is none. People go hungry even for three days. Nobody attends to old people. Nowadays we keep asking if we are human beings or animals on earth. Those with money eat, those without go with no food for days. (Female, 19 years)

Human rights organisations have noted that the government was more concerned with saving the dented image of Kenya by showing that it had rapidly managed to solve its political crisis especially after signing the National Accord. Additionally, it seemed that top on the government agenda was national economic recovery rather than putting in place sufficient resettlement mechanisms that ensured a safe return of the IDPs to their pre-displacement homes or elsewhere. Quite the contrary, the government reduced food rations in order to 'encourage' IDPs to leave camps and used force to evict them from the camps (KHRC 2009) making them suffer a double tragedy evictions by their host community and then by the state. Even when the original camps were closed, the problem of food spilled into the transit and self-help camps due to failed processes of resettlement.

The transit camps were located near the farms of the returnees and this gave some accessibility to their farms. However, as we found, they still faced and feared attacks by their hosts. In one camp, we were informed that one of the IDPs had been attacked with a spear in his farm during the day. It became difficult for some returnees to access their farms and be able to provide food for themselves. On the other hand, the self-help IDPs had bought land in remote areas that did not support farming because the amount of money offered by the government was insufficient to buy more expensive land in arable areas. Thus, whereas government had envisioned an end to the post-election crisis, it became clear that many IDPs still needed relief food but the government had radically reduced the food rations and supply as evidenced in this interview with a 38 year old married female:

> We are given food but it is really delayed. When we were at the show ground (original camp), there was better supply of food, but now we sometimes stay for about three months without supply.
>
> We are only given maize and beans. We do not even get cooking oil to fry the food. The food is distributed per family. Each family may get 10 rations of maize and two

> of beans. If you have a family of six how long does the food last? Just a week! What do you do for the next months? The food is supposed to last for a month but the government sometimes takes three months before they can bring more food.

Interviewer: So what happens to the food that is supposed to be given to you every month?

> You can't know. They skip months and when we try to follow up, we don't get it (the food). So you see we are suffering as parents.

As the above quotes clearly suggest that the ORN resettlement programme did not solve the food problem. IDPs continued to rely on food aid. The conception by the government that IDPs would somehow easily reintegrate and reconstruct their livelihoods was a difficult talk to achieve. For survival, the IDPs supplemented the little food supply with finding work – domestic or farm – in the surrounding community but this was unreliable and cheap. According to the United Nations Development Programme (UNDP 2009), many IDPs had nowhere to go or did not feel secured enough to return home. A Kenya Red Cross Society (KRCS), World Food Programme (WFP) and inter-agency assessment conducted in early September 2008 showed that there were at least 100,000 IDPs in 160 transit sites. Those who had farms were supported with agricultural inputs.

The UNDP also points out, as in the quotes above, that the living conditions in transit sites were worse than in the formal IDP camps managed by the Kenya Red Cross and supported by the humanitarian community. Further, some IDPs who could not return home or were non-farmers went to live in urban informal slums after receiving the Ksh 10,000 from the government. Most of them were found to be living in appalling conditions after exhausting their money.

Human rights organisations such as the KHRC and IDP Network complained to the government over inadequate food supply in the camps. However, the response by some of the government staff was that the government did not have enough resources to feed the IDPs as one senior staff points out:

> Okay, one, you cannot satisfy everybody as a government, it's impossible. Even the funds are not there. The prices of food have also escalated and the ministry of special programme's budget has remained the same; therefore, providing the amount of food that is enough for everybody is not possible. The amount of food we could buy in 2009 is not the amount of food we can buy now (2012) with the escalation of prices... I don't have food here waiting for a disaster to happen so that I can take it, okay? And that now creates friction for us.

The staff noted that there were too high expectations by human rights organisations which the government could not meet. He talked about the inadequate budget allocation to the ministry of special programmes. This official also noted that, as a person responsible for food distribution in his region, he could only rely on the central government in Nairobi for them to plan and bring the food to the region which takes a while due to the red tape involved in government supplies. The failure to provide adequate food constitutes a gross violation of the human rights of IDPs. Further, the expectation that IDPs should find work in the communities to reduce dependence on government is an abdication of the role of government to ensure this provision. Notable is the fact that jobs in the community were inconsistent and inadequate. Additionally, employment was marked by discriminatory and exploitative practices against the IDPs such as poor pay compared to other non-IDP employees, and stigmatisation thus compounding their problems further.

HEALTH AND ACCESS TO HEALTH CARE

Human rights are regarded as fundamental to public health. Health is largely influenced by the physical and social environments in which people live. In many countries such as Kenya, there exists a huge gap between those who enjoy higher standards of health and quality services and those who, for a mix of civil, political, economic, social or cultural services are more vulnerable to ill-health and to inadequate access to health-related services (Gruskin et al 2005). Vulnerable populations such as the IDPs experience dire health risks.

Health standards in the camps were far from ideal. The physical and social environment in the camps, as discussed above, was appalling: poor shelter, pitiable sanitation, lack or shortage of water, inadequate food, insecurity and poor nutrition, scarce clothing and cold/rainy weather coupled with derisory health infrastructure. This combination of factors subjected IDPs to various health effects. According to the internal displacement monitoring centre (IDMC 2008), IDPs were exposed to frequent outbreaks of various diseases such as common colds, waterborne diseases, and diarrhoea. The government took long to set up clinics in the camps. Children were particularly vulnerable to these diseases.

During the interviews, IDPs expressed particular concern for deteriorating health in the camps. Jane, a 66 year old woman, who takes care of three grandchildren, told us of her experiences with health problems in the camp:

> Our main problem here is health; it is hard to find food, health care. Even when a person dies, it is difficult to bury them. Life here is hard. We have nothing we can say is okay. Generally, our life is bad. Let me say, I left my home with no health problems but now I am always being rushed to hospital as if I am dying. How many people have died here, how many are lying in bed sick? They are many. Yet the government is now calm. Like now, if

> you go to tell them that you have lost a family member (died), they will ask "what kind of person? IDP?" I would like them to stop politicising IDP issues; they should know we are human. They should ask themselves, what if they were like us. I am now sick and I was not sick before the conflicts. (Jane, female, 66 years)

Jane attributed her ailing health to lack of food, proper health care, shelter and living conditions in the camp. She was bitter about her experience noting that she did not have health problems before coming to the camp and now she has to keep visiting the hospital for treatment. In addition, she noted that many IDPs went through similar experiences but the government did not help them anymore. Unlike in the formal camps where humanitarian organisations and the government assisted IDPs in accessing health care, in the transit and self-help camps, they were required to pay for health services by themselves but they lacked the resources to do so. Many IDPs lived very far from health facilities and lacked transport and money to pay for health care. Jane wondered why the government was not concerned with their well-being and instead played politics around IDP issues.

Mental health was a problem in the camps. As noted by other scholars (Meintjes, Pillay and Turshen 2002), mental health problems result from the traumas suffered after physical or sexual violence or by economic difficulties. Physical, sexual and mental health are thus inseparable. It must be noted that many IDPs suffered physical injuries including sexual violence which required long term care even after healing physically. Whereas there were more psycho-social support programmes immediately following the violence and before the ORN, these had reduced significantly in the other camps. During this research we interviewed women who had experienced sexual violence during or after the election. Other IDPs had open wounds, burns or mental disturbances, all of which they linked to the political crisis. For example, in an Eldoret camp in

October 2008, we found two mentally ill girls who had been raped before the poll-violence. They did not know where their parents were. A guardian took them under her care in the camp. One of the girls had a huge swelling on her neck and according to their guardian, she was also HIV positive. There had been no medical treatment for them by the time of this study.

In one of the camps in 2011, we talked with an older man in his seventies, husband to Susan, a participant in this study. Susan welcomed Njiru to her house and introduced us to her husband. He repeatedly asked her names and where she had come from. According to his wife, and as told by other participants in that camp, the man had suffered depression due to the evictions that led to the loss of his property during the conflicts. Here is part of Susan's story:

> On that day, I had gone to the shop. But I found that everything had been destroyed. He (husband) was at home. He would have died with his two sons, but they hid him in a ditch. He was a tailor and designed women's clothes. He was also a village elder. Those who came to attack were Luos and Kalenjins and they were vowing to kill him. One of my sons died. He got burnt in the banana trees that we had planted outside the house. He was hiding there but they (attackers) set the bananas on fire and the dry leaves burnt him to death. He and his other son remained in the ditch and then they ran away when the attackers left. He has never seen anything of this sort and it really affected him to see his property getting destroyed. That disturbed him. When we went to the showground (camp), he would wake up in the middle of the night. One night he woke up and told me, 'wake up and tell me what is this you have planned with other people for us to come and live in a tent. This seems to be your plan. The way you keep leaving the camp (when she goes to look for work), it seems you have a plot against me.'

Susan went on to tell Njiru that on many occasions in the camp, her husband had attempted to leave in order to return to their home. But all the camp residents knew about his condition and stopped him from leaving the camp precincts. The fact that the man required constant care limited Susan's capacity to look for work outside the camps to enable her to provide for her family. She had three grandchildren that were in her care. She said that she had lost any hope of finding help for her husband and for the entire family who also relied on her.

What is also important to note here is that long-term mental health care was not a priority in the camps. Further, as some scholars have pointed out many health workers rarely take into consideration mental health issues. They rarely recognise them and hardly make the mentally ill the object of psychological, material or appropriate legal assistance (Meintjes, Pillay and Turshen 2002). Therefore, even though this man has lived with a mental health problem since his days in the original camps where they had free medical care, he was not given adequate support. Additionally, part of the problem is that generally depression is not taken as a serious health problem in the Kenyan society. As such the burden of care for this man fell solely on his wife.

Persons living with HIV were particularly vulnerable. According to the Kenya National AIDS Control Council estimates, some 15,000 of the people displaced by the post-election violence were living with HIV, with about 6,750 in need of ART and 2,550 already on treatment but were not able to access it (Regional Centre for Quality Healthcare 2009; International Organisation for Migration 2013). A Reuters Report (2008) quotes Elisabeth Byrs, a spokeswoman for the UN Office for the Coordination of Humanitarian Affairs in Geneva, as saying that "Without adequate nutrition, water and sanitation, and vital AIDS services, people living with HIV are at risk of succumbing to opportunistic infections and more rapid disease progression". Further the sexual attacks on women and girls in the camps, and sex trade in exchange for food and protection increased their exposure to HIV risks and other sexually transmitted infections. Relief health workers noted that HIV patients were receiving sub-optimal treatment, and tuberculosis, which is particularly harmful for HIV patients, was spreading undetected in the camps.

Women and girls, however, had other specific challenges with reproductive health needs. Female participants reported lack of dignity kits and reproductive health services. Pregnant women were especially vulnerable because they did not have adequate nutrition or access to maternal health services. Immediate humanitarian responses after the violence did not prioritise women's specific needs as the main concern at that time was to protect, shelter and provide food. However, a comprehensive humanitarian response programme involving government and humanitarian agencies was set up and recognised women-specific needs. Thus various agencies, particularly women's organisations including one that Njiru worked for, provide dignity kits to women. Each kit carried sanitary pads, anti-bacterial soap, underwear, towels and washing supplies. But these were not adequate to meet the demands of the number of women and girls who needed them. In addition, a more comprehensive humanitarian response was only available in the formal camps and not in the camps that sprouted during the ORN. The following quotes capture the experiences of some of the women we spoke with:

> When we came here, I had only one pair of underwear. Sometimes, I used to wash it at night so that it is dry in the morning. During the monthly periods, it is very challenging. I remember when I had only one underwear and I could not wash it because I needed it. Now it is better, we got people who gave us some underwear. However, we girls still experience difficulties with pads. We still use old clothing. There is no more help from government or organisations, yet our parents cannot afford to buy pads, they are very expensive.

> The problem we are going through currently is the usual problem involving women (monthly periods) and we do not have anything to use (sanitary towels) at that time. Also we need to have two or more underwear but we only have one and it cannot help especially during that time.

Suggested in the above excerpts, and as repeatedly told by the women we spoke with, menstruation was a difficult period for them. They sometimes used blankets and old pieces of clothing. Young girls missed school during their monthly periods because they did not have sanitary towels. This affected their performance in school.

In addition, women experienced more health risks because of their increased responsibilities in the camps. By virtue of their reproductive role, women are traditionally the guardians of the health of their family members. Therefore, their role to feed their families, coupled with increase in the number of people who were ailing as a result of the conflicts escalated their responsibilities and simultaneously had negative effects on their own health. For example, it was not uncommon for women to report that they did not eat a meal because there was not enough food to feed their families. Further, it is well documented that food insecurity contributes to other serious health risks. The lack of food and of income-generating opportunities to secure food leads to higher rates of prostitution and sexual exploitation among displaced women and girls (Mooney 2005). In this study, participants reported that some women were engaged in sex work in order to meet familial responsibilities. With hardly any possibility to negotiate condom use, the women get exposed to serious health consequences such as HIV infection and other sexually transmitted infections that then inhibit their care giving role thus compounding their problems further.

Recognising the health crisis situation for displaced persons, many agencies responded as part of the wider coordinated comprehensive humanitarian response to the post-election conflicts. The health cluster was led by World Health Organisation (WHO) who coordinated health responses for the IDPs. WHO and other health partners developed a comprehensive response plan at national and provincial level. However, reports from various organisations indicate that health responses were hampered by the complicated dynamics of humanitarian organisations. For example, most of the responses were coordinated through the UN-led cluster approach. However, some organisations such as *Médecins Sans Frontières,* and the International Committee of the Red Cross, are not part of the cluster approach even though they do share data about their activities (IRIN 2008). In addition, some NGOs did not want to be associated with the UN, feeling that they would lose their independence. Also, there were indications that the government had its own parallel response. Indeed, a commissioner with the Kenya National Commission on Human Rights (KNCHR) observed that the response to the post-election IDP situation was fragmented. There was a lot of corruption and the sick IDPs in the fields were not able to access hospitals. Women too did not receive reproductive health services (IRIN 2008).

While we discuss violence against women and its consequences in greater details in chapter five, it is important to note that the issues of food, health and violence are not unrelated. Without access to means of survival and hopes of building lives of dignity, the consequences of the violence that led people to these camps simply extend over long periods of time. In other words, violence leads to broken lives. Furthermore, efforts that are made to address the general health and security of the people in the camps affect people who are victims of violence and those who are not in somewhat different ways. For example, government and relief workers set up mobile clinics in camps to ensure access to health. However, the lack of coordination, sometimes duplication of efforts meant that response efforts in health were fragmented. Additionally, in many instances these outreach services faced several challenges, including staff shortages and ethnic animosity (Health Rights Advocacy Forum 2008). What was at stake here was the health of the men and women living in camps.

The health of the IDPs was even more at stake at the implementation of the ORN resettlement programme. The implementation of the programme meant that provision of health scaled down tremendously as part of the scheme to facilitate resettlement plans. Yet, there were no mechanisms to ensure that, for example, people in need of accessing healthcare had the financial capacity to do so before they could rebuild their lives once more. As noted elsewhere, the government incentive for resettlement was inadequate and was heavily criticised for insufficiency. Consequently, in the transit and self-help camps, health problems persisted, yet unlike in the formal camps, there was no coordinated humanitarian response. Some camps were far away from hospitals and IDPs had to make their own transport arrangements and medical expenses while they did not have a sustainable livelihood. Many lacked the financial resources to do so in a country that has no national health insurance plan. There was very little support from organisations too. Therefore, as the study found, many men and women complained of health neglect. Women, especially, bore the burden of taking care of the ill family members sacrificing their own health.

ACCESS TO EDUCATION

Education is vital for the full realisation of an individual's potential. It is also critical to a country's social and economic advancement. Recognising this, the UN Millennium Development Goal 2 sets a universal primary education target for all nations by 2015. In 2003, the Kenyan government introduced a 'free'[10] primary school education policy. Free primary education was seen as crucial to the attainment of this goal. This policy has, however, faced sharp criticisms such as the mismanagement of resources and ineffective implementation that leaves many deserving children out of school.

The post-election violence caused significant losses to the education of the affected population in particular, and to the country more broadly. Schools were burnt down in some communities as part of the evictions. Teachers, students and parents fled as a result of the conflicts. In the camps, various agencies and organisations have noted that humanitarian responses to enable the affected school children to resume learning were slow and ineffective. The lack of teachers and infrastructure hampered this process. It was also difficult for the young boys and girls who were in high schools or who were waiting to join high school after their 8 years of primary education. High school education is not free. Further, it was more difficult to find local high schools because the pupils could not go back to their high schools in the community from which they fled. As a result, many children delayed or dropped out of school altogether. During his 2011 visit to Kenya, the UN Special Rapporteur on the Human Rights of IDPs found that schools were often in deplorable conditions; there were not enough teachers, and parents were unable to meet the costs of education (OHCHR, February 2012).

The main education challenges for the IDPs still living in camps at the time of this study were twofold: (a) access and (b) discriminatory practices in schools. The following excerpt from Tabitha in 2011, mother of 10 children some of who have their own children, depicts this:

> One of the things that has contributed to our problems is the discrimination of our children in schools. When a child is in school they are asked "are you from the camp?" They are insulted because they are from the camp. One of my grandchildren told me "grandmother, I don't like to admit that I am from the camp because we are

> despised". You see, ever since we were at the showground, our children were not put in schools; they were given tents as classrooms instead. Our children lagged behind in education but God has helped them. Even here in this camp, we still have many challenges such as paying examination fee. Sometimes the child cannot go to school because there is no food. If there is no food, how can the child concentrate in school? When they miss school because of lack of food, the next time they go to school they are told (by administration) to go back to the camp. They are told "you come from the camp, you get free food, and how can you not have food". So we have many problems . . . In fact, when I tried to find a school for my daughter that is near our camp, the head teacher told me that all his classrooms were filled up and I should find a different school...I had to find another school that is far from here. So you see, our children are discriminated against until they sometimes drop out of school.

This quote demonstrates several challenges in access to education that many of the study participants, particularly parents who had school children talked about. One problem exemplified here is lack of infrastructure. Tabitha points out that at the showground (original camp) the IDP children learnt in tents. Of course, in situations of conflict-induced displacement, schools often get destroyed or damaged. In camps, therefore, schools tend to be makeshift and only offer primary education. They lacked inadequate staff and other essentials such as blackboards. Also, because they only offered primary education, those in high schools delayed re-entry to the available schools. When the original camps closed, IDPs experienced difficulties trying to find schools for the children in the communities they returned to. Further, increasing number of pupils in schools puts pressure on the existing – and often inadequate – infrastructure that characterises many public schools in Kenya, particularly those in the rural areas.

Tabitha was turned away from one school because there was no space for her daughter. She felt this was discrimination because she was a displaced person. From our perspective, it is possible that the school turned her away for lack of resources. On the other hand, from Tabitha's perspective not being able to get her daughter admitted into a school is a personal disaster that she attributes to her IDP status.

Second, as Tabitha notes, the children faced double discrimination – by the school administration and other children in school. She talked about children being turned away from school if they had missed school the previous day. According to Tabitha, the administration did not see how an IDP who is supposed to receive free food from government, cannot have food. This showed lack of understanding of food security in the camps. Children from the camps were also treated differently by other school children. As Tabitha's grandchild tells her, "Grandma, I don't like to admit that I am from the camp because we are despised". This implies that the IDP label carried a stigma and may have strained relationships between some IDP and non-IDP children thus affecting their education.

The third predicament is distance. Tabitha's daughter's school was far from the camp. She was concerned about the distance that her daughter walked to and from the school. Given that sometimes the children went without a meal, it became difficult for them to walk far distances to school. Security was another major concern for parents whose children had to walk for miles to go to school. For example, another participant pointed out sexual violence, especially for the girl children. To ensure the safety of their daughters, she and other mothers walked their daughters to school early in the morning because they had to pass through a grazing field that had previously reported various forms of violence – harassment and rape – by men grazing their animals in the open field. Similarly, most evenings, if it began to get dark before the girls were back home, the mothers went to fetch them from school.

The fourth concern was affordability. Tabitha reported that she had difficulties raising money for examination fee. It must be noted that even if primary school education is free, the hidden costs (Ngwacho et al 2013) make education inaccessible to people without adequate financial resources. In addition to this, because only primary education is free, parents have to pay full tuition fees for secondary education. Due to loss of livelihood, it becomes difficult for parents to meet these costs. We asked parents about access to education bursaries, a scheme introduced as one of the safety-nets to cushion the poor and vulnerable groups (Njeru and Orodho 2003). Their responses indicated that they felt discriminated against in the bursary scheme; although IDPs stood qualified for the scheme, they did not receive any help while, as they complained, other non-displaced children had accessed bursaries. Njeru and Orodho (2003) in their study on 'education financing in Kenya', critiqued the bursary scheme for poor quality of service, bad governance and management weaknesses. Faced with such difficulties, many children in the camps did not proceed to secondary school and this also raised other concerns for the IDPs, as expressed in the following excerpt.

> I had my own cows. I had everything. Now I cannot educate my children. These children are very intelligent. This woman's grandchild (pointing to another woman) passed very well but she cannot afford to take the child to school. Now what do they want us to do, we are Kenyans. They have cut short our years. If you walk around here you will find that many women are sick. Let me ask you, if we cannot feed ourselves how can we afford to take these children to school. Of those two, what is the choice? It is sad to see our children's future destroyed.

This illustration contrasts the lives of IDPs before and after the violence. Whereas during pre-conflict period they were able to educate their children, this was now a challenge. As a consequence, this participant noted that women's health was at risk because they not only struggled to feed their families but also had to educate them. Important to note is the fact that within the Kenyan context, it is mostly women who worry about school fees and other education related expenses for their children. Further, due to the nature of jobs that IDPs were able to access in the surrounding communities, women had more job opportunities than men. As noted by one of the participants, "these men have no jobs, they cannot do house work and there are no big farms". This gender differentiation of roles implied that women were almost entirely responsible for meeting the needs of their families including the education of their children because men would not find work as domestic workers. Yet, these were the types of jobs more commonly available to the IDPs in the host communities. As such this participant felt that "they (government) have cut our years".

Fifth, another challenge with access to education relates to loss of identification documents. Reports from various organisations such as the ICJ and KNCHR (2012) and IDMC (2012) pointed out that displacement resulted in loss of important identification documents that are required for school enrolment. Without these, education is compromised. The process of replacing these documents in Kenya is often long and frustrating due to bureaucratic processes and sometimes results in corruption. At times, it requires that IDPs return to their places of origin (IDMC 2012) which may not be in their interest given their experience in those communities during the election violence.

Within the framework of these challenges, the consequences of missing out on education cannot be underestimated. As noted earlier, the goal of education is to enable individuals to develop their full potential and more broadly contribute to the social and economic development of their environment. It is, however, clear that children affected by the election conflicts immensely missed out on these opportunities as captured here.

> Those who have finished their primary schooling also have many problems. They cannot continue with school, they are idle. On some days, they will find work but it is not enough. That is why you find many of them engage in drugs and alcohol . . . For the girls, it is worse because they are selling their bodies in order to make money. Men, both within and outside the camp, are actually using (exploiting) them. There are many teenage pregnancies in the camp. This is of course a burden for the older women, because you have to take care of both your daughter and her child. Some girls have left the camp to work as live-in domestic workers in towns and leave us with their young children.

This quote allows us to see the tough choices that IDPs have to make. Generally, people aspire to go to school in order to escape poverty in the longer term. However, for IDPs this aspiration is cut short. Given that pursuing education is not an option for them because they cannot afford it; they are faced with tough choices of coping with their situation. Some turn to drugs and alcohol as coping mechanisms or the girls sell their bodies in order to survive. But this compounds their problem even further. For example, when young girls become pregnant, they are caught in the trap of further cycles of poverty. At the same time, the issues we have raised in this chapter regarding the experiences of living in camps are of particular concern and raise critical questions regarding their aspirations for education. For instance, what would an education do for them given their living conditions? What makes more sense, to remain in school or to put food on the table? For the IDPs, these are tough choices. In light of the quote above, it is safe to argue that this exclusion and marginalisation of displaced children in terms of education further disadvantage their lives now and in the future. The missed opportunities in education are a recipe for a perpetuation of a cycle of poverty and vulnerability for these children, who at no fault of their own have to bear consequences of battles of political supremacy.

CONCLUDING THOUGHTS

When people flee from violence, the general human rights approach expects that some aspects of their lives will improve because they have left the context in which violence occurred. However, this chapter has analysed the grounded realities of all the additional challenges the IDPs face because of insufficient understanding of their life conditions and inadequate resources to help them build lives of dignity (the stated objective of human rights interventions). Even though human rights – and the political, civil, economic, social and cultural edifice that are supposed to ensure lives of human dignity – are perceived to be universal, the structural conditions in the camps show that only a few human rights standards are met. While scholars have continued to debate the universality of human rights focusing on the extent to which these rights match with or violate the cultural norms or legal framework in a country, little attention has been paid to the structural conditions that exist in camps that prevent access to almost any type of right. In this chapter, we have described violations of the right to adequate housing, safe drinking water and sanitation, food, education and health and illustrated how fleeing from one kind of violence – itself a failure to ensure peaceful conditions of life – lead individuals into situations that can further prolong the impact of the initial cycles of violence that caused them to flee, and additionally, exacerbate their vulnerability to violence and weaken their access to human rights. Thus, fleeing to camps does not make their lives violence-free. We also hinted at some aspects of violence against women in this chapter but discuss this in greater details in the next chapter.

CHAPTER FOUR

Violence against Women

Experiences of Women and Young Girls in IDP Camps

In February (2008), while in this camp, a GSU officer lied to a girl who had lost her tent that he would give her one. The officer took the girl to his house and raped her and cut her private parts. The girl's private parts were badly mutilated. She reported to the police station and was later taken to hospital but the GSU officer (Male, 38 years) *was not arrested.*

I severally heard allegations of service providers soliciting for sex but people would not come out to give evidence. We over-trusted the Red Cross officials not knowing they were causing more problems. We trusted that they would take care of girls. Churches did a better job. (Provincial administrator)

Here in the camp, women now think they are equal to men because men cannot provide and they both depend on aid. In our former homes men were the head of the family but here in the camp it's like both husband and wife are heads. This has led to no respect between wives and husbands and

> *hence fights. Men do not go to work and because of this they have no money. When a man comes home and the wife asks for salt and he fails to provide, this makes men feel bad and it leads to quarrels.* (Married male, 26 years)

We start this chapter with the accounts above because they raise pertinent questions about violence against women (VAW) in camps. First, in reading these quotations we ask, how is violence linked to the material conditions of IDPs living in camps? What makes it possible for persons charged with the responsibility of protecting and providing services to internally displaced women living in camps sexually abuse them? What does this tell us about the layers of vulnerability that these women experience? Second, we ask how is violence against women in the camps conceptualised (by the state) and how does this conceptualisation inform the ways in which policies and interventions on VAW are implemented. These questions and more form the subject matter of this chapter. But, first, we provide some clarification on the focus of the chapter.

As noted in the introduction, this book is about the daily life experiences of internally displaced persons in the camps. This chapter specifically pays attention to the continuing violence against women that occurs in the camps. We do not specifically focus on violence against women during the post-election conflicts but will draw on it to explicate the continuum of violence that women experience during and post-conflict situations (Meintjes, Pillay and Turshen 2001). It is thus not a reading on the use of 'sexual violence as a weapon of war'.[11] This does not in any way discredit the fact that sexual violence was part and parcel of the election violence in Kenya which caused serious harm on women (and men). We emphasise that it is indeed necessary to recognise and record this trauma for the sake of both history and for enhanced social understanding of the trauma caused by election conflicts (Weaver 2010). This chapter, therefore, takes account of how women (and men) who experienced egregious harms during the 2007-08 post-election conflicts continue to experience further forms of violence in the camps which are supposed to offer them protection. This allows us to see the multiple layers of vulnerability and violence that women and young girls experience. In addition, as with Sideris (2001), we examine the social context in which women are subject to violations in order to promote an understanding of how specific conditions affect the ways in which "women interpret their violation, create the limits and possibilities to challenge inequalities they experience, and promote the necessity of superiority and control in men" (p.144), and therefore, also challenging the attainment of women's human rights.

As implied above, we expect this chapter to contribute to debates on the continuous violence that women experience from the private sphere of their homes (before fleeing camp) to public spaces (camps). Women and human rights organisations in Kenya have reported on the occurrence of VAW during and after the PEV (examples: CREAW 2008; ICJ and KHRC 2008, 2009, 2012). They point out that women and girls continue to bear heavy consequences of the post-election conflicts in the forms of sexual, physical and psychological abuse and discrimination. In the end, this chapter provides for a theorisation of women's experiences of violence. We have chosen to focus on physical experiences of violence – sexual and physical. In attempting to answer some of the questions, we problematise the private/public codification of VAW and the treatment of 'public' spaces – such as camps – as private spheres by the state apparatus thus leading to neglect by government interventions. In our analysis of data, therefore, we employ a broader conceptualisation of VAW in line with current debates in human rights. We examine the ways in which VAW in camps is integrally linked to policies, institutional arrangements and practices, including cultural norms and patriarchy that endow this violence. Consequently, this chapter links VAW to the material conditions discussed in the previous chapters and enables us to analyse women's own negotiations of their marginality within the framework of human rights and of the responsibility of the state to protect internally displaced persons.

We begin with a broad overview of the conceptualisation of violence against women. This draws on the international level processes that pushed for a broader view of VAW. We then provide a brief analysis on the existing legal framework on women's rights. Following this, we examine intimate partner violence in the camps, highlighting how women perceive the violence. Further, we explore sexual violence experienced by young girls in the camps and the consequences of this violence – family violence; teenage pregnancy, abortion and abortion related complications; and the consequent burden and cycles of violence in their families. We finally examine the use of power by persons, assigned with the responsibility to protect or provide humanitarian aid to displaced persons, who coerce women into sex for exchange of the essential services. Our overall goal is to provide an understanding of how the failure to protect and ensure the human rights of internally displaced women and girls increases their vulnerability to violence in the camps. First, let us conceptualise violence against women in the broader sense.

CONCEPTUALISING VIOLENCE AGAINST WOMEN

At the 1993 UN conference on Human Rights in Vienna, global activism by women drew attention to the issue of VAW. The 1993 UN Declaration of Elimination of Violence against Women defined VAW as "any act of gender-based violence that results in, or is likely to result in, physical, sexual or mental harm or suffering to women, including threats of such acts, coercion or arbitrary deprivation of liberty, whether occurring in public or in private life" (United Nations 1993). The 1995 Platform for Action of the Fourth World Conference on Women in Beijing included a section on VAW to encompass gender based violence in the family or in the community or perpetrated by the state that results in physical, sexual, psychological harm or suffering to women in private or public life (Merry 2006). This definition expanded the understanding of VAW far beyond the ambit of homes and intimate relationship violence within private spheres to violence which occurs within a continuum from private spaces to public contexts. Thus the structural circumstances that promote a continuum of violence including street harassment, violence within families, violence in times of conflict and sexual violence became visible (Ertürk and Purkayastha 2012). These expanding definitions enable us to draw attention to hitherto neglected areas of society in which VAW occurs, such as the IDP camps in Kenya.

Scholarly research on VAW has pointed out how private and public spheres are linked to shape this violence (Bennett 2005; Britton 2006; Ertürk and Purkayastha 2012). Importantly, the UN office of Special Rapporteur on VAW has pushed for a definition of VAW that goes beyond individuals and cultures to link it to institutional arrangements in the society that shape this violence. VAW is thus conceptualised along a continuum from the intimate partner violence that occurs in the private spheres to community and violence by the state. Yet, in spite of this definition, current practices in addressing VAW still largely treat it in isolation from structural circumstances that determine this violence. We use this broader definition of violence that is more consistent with current thinking in human rights because it lends us an opportunity to examine how various forms of structural level violence continue to allow bodily assaults – sexual and physical – experienced by internally displaced women living in the camps in Kenya.

WOMEN'S RIGHTS INSTRUMENTS IN KENYA

Theoretically, the Kenya government is committed to safeguarding women and girls from all forms of violence, particularly structural violence that is linked to other forms of violence. As we discussed in the introduction, the role of government in addressing violence against women is tied to the ratification and adoption of various international protocols such as the Committee on the Elimination of Discrimination against Women (CEDAW), Declaration on the Elimination of Violence Against Women (DEVAW), Universal Declaration on Human Rights (UDHR); International Covenant on Economic, Social, and Cultural Rights (ICESCR) and the Covenant on Civil and Political Rights (ICCPR). Kenya is also a party to the African Commission on Human and Peoples Rights (ACHPR). Additionally, there are legal provisions at national level that protect women and girls from violence, such as the constitution and the penal code. Kenya has in place a National Gender Policy and a National Gender and Equality Commission. Despite all these legal provisions, Kenya has yet to eliminate or significantly reduce VAW that is understood within a historical and cultural context of traditional patriarchal domination, colonial rule and introduction of new economic and social structures that disrupted kinship relations (Federation of Women Lawyers-Kenya 2002; CREAW 2006), neo-liberal policies and participation in the global market economy. The government largely adopts a 'non-interference policy' on VAW since violence is considered a domestic affair or an issue for elders in the community to deal with. This 'silent policy' has to be, however, understood in the context of the state's role in gender construction that perpetuates VAW (Brush 2003; Majstorovic and Lassen 2011). On the contrary, addressing VAW requires a consideration of the intersecting factors of social, economic and political structures that instigate this violence (Ertuk and Purkayastha 2012; True 2012). With this view of VAW in mind, we present the daily life experiences of physical violence for women and young girls in the camps.

INTIMATE PARTNER VIOLENCE

SEXUAL AND PHYSICAL VIOLENCE

We have argued that political and economic (structural) violence have a direct bearing on women's bodily experiences with violence. We have also noted elsewhere in the last chapter that women were particularly vulnerable to abuse. For example, Sara, one of the research participants, compared her life before and after the post-election conflicts. She sadly pointed out during our interview, "Things are not the same anymore". Poverty and the concurrent problems of hunger, poor housing conditions and sanitation, deficient or inadequate access to even basic health care including reproductive health for women, child malnourishment, school drop-out among young boys and girls, have shaped violence at the family level in various ways.

One dimension of how violence has manifested itself at the family level is through sexual and physical abuse of women by their partners, as Sara narrated:

> My husband beat me up because I refused to have sex with him. He came back home at night drunk and was loudly demanding for sex in the presence of the children. Our tents are very small and we have three children but he still wants me to have sex. Some couples quarrel until they throw each other out of their tents like my neighbours did.

This excerpt illustrates many layers of violence in displacement camps that are results of political conflicts. These include poor housing and overcrowding in tents, conditions which offered no privacy for marital/sexual relations as children slept in the same room with their parents. Yet, male partners forcefully demanded for sex from their wives disregarding the presence of children in the same room. Additionally, physical abuse often accompanied sexual violence. Sara reported that her husband beat her because she refused to have sex with him. In this connection, Erturk and Purkayastha (2012: 145) point out that the state's "policy of non-intervention in the private sphere has often been the domain of male supremacy". Even 'private'[12] space in the camps becomes problematic such as in crowded, tented camp conditions as exemplified by Sara when she notes that other couples fought in full glare and knowledge of their neighbours. The lack of privacy for marital/sexual relations coupled with women's subordinate status in society rendered Sara vulnerable to abuse by her husband.

It must be noted that VAW, as experienced by women in this camp, is embedded in cultural understandings of gender and sexuality within the marital institution in Kenya where men primarily enjoy rights over their wives' bodies. In almost all traditional Kenyan societies, the male spouse was regarded as the supreme head of the family, the provider of food and security. Under this patriarchal system, women were regarded as subservient to the male. Masculinity was defined by competitiveness, aggression, independence and suppression of emotion. These traits and social practices rendered forms of male dominance acceptable and helped maintain it. On the other hand, femininity was associated with traits such as passivity, complicity, dependence and sentimentality, depicting weakness, subordination and lower status. Further, a woman had little power to participate in family and clan decision-making processes. Even today, these gendered inequalities persist and are continuously reproduced discursively (though sometimes challenged) through language, religion and other social practices. This negative stereotyping is an effective way of silencing women and leads to creation of an image of powerless, submissive and inferior group (Abudi, Yieke and Kitete 2011). Therefore, a society where the balance of power makes it difficult for women to negotiate sexual practices (when, where, how) within marriage, leaves women's bodies at risk of violence from their partners.

The power imbalance ensures that forced sex and consequent physical assault remain silenced in the spheres of the family and often women blame themselves or find ways to rationalise the actions of their partners. Sara reported that her husband loudly demanded sex because "he came back home drunk". This rationalisation of men's behaviour was also evident amongst other participants as Maria observed, "Men are affected by the post-election conflict until sometimes they just drink alcohol. They do not drink because they want to, they do so because of many problems we face here, my sister". This implies that women should understand the reasons that lead to their husband's drinking habits and the consequences of this drinking-sexual or physical abuse as told by Rosa:

> Eh! Couples here separate and this is caused by those problems (discussed earlier in the interview). Sometimes wives do not understand how things are. They think that they are like they used to be before (the conflicts) when they would wake up and tell their husbands that they need money for sugar and soap. But now when women ask for those things, it becomes a quarrel. These quarrels have been brought about by problems. So today you hear that some couples have marital problems, you hear they have fought and things like that.

These quotes demonstrate that the participants made links between political conflicts that sent them to the camp, current socio-economic conditions in the camps, the drinking behaviour of their husbands and physical and sexual violence. These women associated their experiences of violence with failure of the government to resettle them whereas in Kenya, cultural norms within marriage that expect women to internalise, justify and silence abuse were not brought to the fore. Neither did they talk about their right to protection from sexual or physical abuse by partners. This implies that these women played their role as wives – a term that often connotes property of the male 'bought' through payment of bride price which some male members have used as a justification for control over their wives. No wonder that the majority of women emphatically confirmed that they would not report violence to the police or anyone in authority. This was either because they had learnt to live with it and ignore their partners, or the cases of violence were not serious, or there was no one to report to or there would be no action taken against the men thus leading to more problems for the women. As expressed by Rosa that, "Sometimes there is even no need to waste time going to the police, nothing will happen. It would just create more tension in the house. You would rather spend that time looking for food". When the women mentioned "haki yetu" (our right), they undoubtedly referred to the right to own land, as promised by the government, in order to better their lives. This they hoped would reduce violence.

In Kenya, women are primarily responsible for agricultural production and cultivation. However, without rights to land, women are unable to feed themselves and their families and provide access to shelter, education and healthcare. The question of women's control and access to land has to be seen in historical context. In pre-colonial Kenya, the role of women and girls was to farm the family land (owned communally), harvest and sell farm produce. This gave women control and access to land and ensured some economic empowerment from the sale of produce. However, in colonial Kenya, the British redistributed land and introduced cash crop farming. Women were particularly affected by this system as they lost access and control of the land for they were no longer able to produce and sell subsistence food and became more and more economically dependent on men. This led to the intensification of domestic patriarchy reinforced by colonial social institutions (McKenzie 1990). As colonialism continued, the perceived importance of female agricultural contribution to the household diminished as their vital role in food production was overshadowed by the more lucrative male-controlled cash crop cultivation. The growth of commercial crop production and the introduction of private land rights adversely affected women's access to land (McKenzie 1990). Despite this, gender relations have not been unilinear; they are linked in complex ways with shifts in the political economy of Kenya and household differentiation (Francis 1995). Thus, the question of gender equality and land rights for women remains important even as these rights are currently guaranteed in the new 2010 Kenyan Constitution. Women bear the burden of provision for their families. It is in this context of land rights that the women in camps demanded quick resettlement and silenced violence.

Therefore, the endurance of intimate partner violence in the camp has to be seen in the context of myriad factors. These include the social acceptance of violence, unequal power relations between men and women manifested in beliefs and values that promote male superiority and the objectification of female as property owned by male; failure of government institutions to ensure basic life conditions in camps, lack of resettlement of IDPs and ensuring land rights, lack of prioritisation of violence by both women and government, laxity of police in prosecuting perpetrators of violence, low levels of community sensitisation on existing laws on the rights of women, and a culture that blames the victim for violence meted on them and abhors reportage – particularly of close family members. Evidently, these factors allow for further cycles of VAW to occur in the camp.

YOUNG GIRLS' EXPERIENCE WITH SEXUAL VIOLENCE AND EXPLOITATION

Another dimension of violence that we explored relates to sexual exploitation of young school-age girls, particularly those who discontinue school because their parents cannot afford to pay for it. As noted in the previous chapter, there is wide recognition of education as a basic right and Kenya has a free primary school education policy which covers tuition fees. The detachment of IDPs from their past livelihoods makes it difficult for parents and guardians to afford various school related expenses such as uniforms, books and other levies not covered in the policy. Additionally, parents have to pay tuition and other expenses for secondary school. This means that many children in camps miss out on education.

Kenya defines a child as anybody under the age of 18 years. There are laws providing for child rights and child protection, most commonly the Children's Act. These rights are also enshrined in the Constitution under the bill of rights and in the penal code. They include the right to life, education, health care, protection from sexual exploitation and harmful cultural rites that are likely to negatively affect the child's development. Girls are more vulnerable to violence. The women and child rights movement has led to criminalisation of acts that were traditionally considered a norm such as teenage marriage and (consequent) pregnancy even though some communities still unlawfully practise child marriage, often fuelled by poverty. The living conditions in the camps, including being out of school, make girls susceptible to various forms of violence, such as sexual exploitation and concomitant teenage pregnancies.

During our visits, we often found many children in the camp because they were not in school. The women we spoke with narrated problems experienced by these children, particularly girls, as Maria observed:

> Those (boys and girls) who have finished their primary schooling also have many problems . . . For the girls, it is worse because they are selling their bodies in order to make money. Men, both within and outside the camp, are actually using them. There are many teenage pregnancies and many young families in the camp.

As illustrated in the excerpt, young girls have sexual relationships primarily for economic exchange. It is important to note that sexual exploitation occurs where local social norms allow for such behaviour to occur. Betha concurred with the above quote noting that,

> I know a young girl here, she has three children . . . This place is like a town (prostitution). They do it day and night, in the maize field and the abandoned airstrip; there is no need for lodging.

Sadly, economic desperation and living conditions in the camp override consideration of these relationships as exploitative. As a result, there have been very few arrests of sexual abuse (rape) of minors. Even in cases of rape, as Ruth, an NGO participant told me, are rarely reported:

> I have dealt with about 3 or 4 cases of GBV (Gender Based Violence). I have worked there (camp) for almost 2 years and even over. A minor was abused by her uncle. We reported to the police and the man was arrested. The three cases which I have come across there, the men were arrested. We just got them arrested. And the women, sometimes they don't say (report). All what we normally see is a lot of abortions . . . I think they have seen more of problems and they find as if they will never overcome that problem and they tend now to stay with it. It has become part of their life. And we really don't know what we can do about it.

As the three quotes above demonstrate, sexual abuse is "part of women's life" in the camp. We have noted earlier that cultural norms and inaccessible justice systems inhibit women from reporting cases of abuse. In addition, an official from the gender unit at the local police station noted that amongst other challenges such as underfunding, "the unit is under police jurisdiction making it inaccessible to the public". Attitudes associated with gender discriminatory practices in police stations discouraged reporting of violence. Thus, sexual violence becomes a 'normal' physical experience for the young girls. As Ruth suggests, women in the camp "have seen more problems". This means that there are other more significant problems than physical assaults that take priority in their lives. Consequently, they do not report assault and exploitation of younger girls. Many of these girls are minors under Kenyan law. And, as stipulated in the Sexual Offences Act (2006), the offenders should be punished for engaging in sex with a minor.

Quite the contrary, the consequences of normalising and condoning sexual exploitation are borne by the bodies of these young girls. One of these consequences is unplanned pregnancies and related risks of abortion.

Teenage pregnancy and abortions, as highlighted in the last two excerpts, are of major concern to both women and some of the NGO representatives that we interviewed. Teenage pregnancy is not only a violation of the young girls' rights, because it is fuelled by poverty, but it also diminishes their life chances. In addition, when abortions occur, they are carried out clandestinely because abortion is illegal in Kenya. Sometimes abortion results in dire complications placing a higher financial burden on the mothers of these girls who have to meet post-abortion care costs. On the other hand, teenage pregnancies increase the likelihood of violence in the family, as Betha told us:

> Sometimes there are disagreements between couples over how to deal with the children's behaviour. Or sometimes a man beats up his daughter for becoming pregnant because she is adding an extra burden to the already destitute conditions. That is one of the reasons they (daughters) leave to seek employment as domestic house helps in towns and cities and send money back to us to care for their babies. The money they send back also helps us a little.

Betha's account demonstrates to us the never-ending cycles of violence that girls living in this camp experience as a result of the post-election conflicts. They drop out of school due to financial problems, engage in sexual relationships for money, some get pregnant and become susceptible to further physical abuse by their fathers for being pregnant. Moreover, as noted in the quote, some young mothers have to leave their babies in search of employment where they work as minors especially as domestic workers in the urban centres. It is worth noting that in Kenya, employment of minors often under exploitative conditions as domestic workers is not uncommon (International Labour Organisation and Kenya National Bureau of Statistics 2012). The quote, thus, highlights the interwoven nature of the various levels and forms of violence that these girls experience. This in fact further questions the schisms between private and public spheres of violence; the government almost neglects VAW that occurs in "domestic" spheres in the IDP camps. Further, violence is hardly seen as linked to the material realities of women and men in the camps.

COERCION, ABUSE OF POWER AND VIOLENCE

It was apparent in this study that some women were engaged in sex in exchange for goods and services that were provided to internally displaced persons – clothing, security or health care services. Looking at the material conditions in the camps, we were able to understand how women participated in this exchange with people who could provide these goods, such as the humanitarian workers and police officers. Women and young girls were coerced into giving sexual favours because there were no other options that would enable them to access these basic services in the camps. This 'survival sex' constitutes a form of sexual violence. Coercion occurred at the structural level where those in positions of power, with access to goods and services that women needed, demanded sex as a precondition for provision of services. Some of our participants reported that in the early days of living in the camps, aid workers and law enforcers were main perpetrators of sexual violence in the camps. The following statement from a female in one of the camps illustrates the cases of abuse of power and sexual violence:

> It is true, you will find that sometimes women and girls sleep with the NGO workers here or the police. What do

> they do? If you go to tell them that you need this and that, they don't give you immediately. They start talking to you in a different manner (sexually), and many women give in because they need to live. It is a problem here, but there is nothing we can do. Our young girls especially are selling themselves.

In other cases, as reported by this male participant, women and young girls were raped by those who were supposed to protect them:

> In February, in this camp a GSU officer raped a girl. This girl had lost her tent and went to the officer for help. Somehow, the officer took the girl to his house and raped her and cut her private parts. The girl's private parts were badly mutilated. She reported to the police station and was later taken to hospital. The officer was never arrested.

Several agencies and organisations, particularly those focusing on women's rights did report on sexual exploitation and abuse by humanitarian workers in the camps. For example, the Women's Commission for Refugee Women and Children (WCRWC) in their September 2008 report noted that:

> Sexual exploitation was also a major issue and one that did not appear to be diminishing. Service providers and focus group participants raised concern over this issue, as those in positions of power were demanding sexual favours in exchange for commodities, even from younger girls. Young women in a focus group discussion in Kitale Showground noted that girls as young as 12 and 14 were engaged in sex for services; moreover, bribery was widespread. The common response was that personal items, including oil, undergarments, soap, lotion and perfume, were prompting women and girls to engage in

> sex. Perpetrators included police, businessmen and doctors outside the camp, camp leaders and most importantly, humanitarian volunteers who were overseeing sections of the camps (2008:7).

Sexual Exploitation and Abuse (SEA) by humanitarian workers is an important consideration in any humanitarian framework worldwide. Indeed, it is a critical component in the training of the workers. As pointed out by the Commission, there seemed to be high levels of planning on how to prevent sexual violence, including sexual exploitation and abuse by humanitarian workers at the national level, but still these efforts were found to be least at the field level. Further, they reported poor security measures and received "numerous disturbing reports of sexual exploitation and abuse by humanitarian workers, police and others" (WCRWC 2008: 1). As a result of lack of or low efforts to prevent sexual abuse by those in positions of power, the perpetrators were not reported or punished. An interview with a provincial administrator revealed this:

> I severally heard of allegations of service providers soliciting for sex but people would not come out to give evidence. We over trusted the Red Cross officials not knowing that they were causing more problems. We trusted that they would take care of girls; churches did a better job.

What we see in these excerpts is that women and young girls may be unwilling to report because this may have consequences for their material survival in the camps. Further, it would be difficult for a woman to prove that they were coerced into sex in exchange of commodities or services. It is also possible that the victims did not know that they could report or in fact where to report sexual exploitation because unlike rape, it may not be taken with any seriousness at all.

These accounts reflect various levels of barriers to reporting and disclosure of gender violence that operate at the personal, societal and criminal justice system levels. At the personal level, as stated here, many victims are afraid that if they report, the perpetrator will kill them, harm their children or other family members. Some victims may be ashamed or embarrassed to report and believe that they deserve to be abused. Others may fail to report violence if they are economically dependent on their men and afraid of losing this financial support or anticipating further violence from their spouses especially for those who are already in unions where there are cycles of abuse. At the societal level, one of the important factors that hinders reporting is silencing violence through victim blaming. Male victims remain silent because of cultural attitudes that see male abuse as a sign of weakness thus victimising them further. These create a climate of tolerance and promote social passivity making it difficult for victims to report.

At the criminal justice level, victims face difficulties in accessing justice due to absence of an effective link to the judicial system. As a requirement to meet the international standards for measuring violence, particularly VAW, Kenya has, however, made efforts to create gender desks and units at police stations and to train the police officers in charge of the desks. It also created gender focal points in various ministries. Thus, the government is committed to addressing gender violence at this level. As for the gender desks in police stations, many are, however, dysfunctional due to inadequate resource allocation and shortage of police officers trained on gender issues (Ombwori 2009). Additionally, women especially face obstacles due to gender-based discrimination in the administration of justice and patriarchal attitudes and cultural norms that condone VAW and discourage reporting (CREAW 2008). Therefore, there is no guarantee that reporting will lead to an arrest and subsequent conviction. These factors make the gender desks counterproductive. They also obstruct women from accessing other specialist services. Thus, given these weaknesses in preventing sexual abuse, gender discrimination may have led to tolerance for all forms of sexual violence in the camps.

CONCLUDING THOUGHTS

In this chapter we have highlighted the physical experiences of violence by women and young girls in the camps. We focused on intimate partner violence and the sexual exploitation of young girls whose experiences of violence are narrated through their mothers. Finally, we examined how people in positions of power, and who are responsible for providing services and protection to internally displaced persons took advantage of their positions to sexually exploit and abuse women and young girls, sometimes by force.

In examining these issues, we find that several social structural factors permitted the occurrence of violence against women in the camps. These include: economic disadvantages arising from the women's displaced status; ineffective mechanisms by different actors – government, humanitarian agencies – for reporting experiences of violence, gender and power inequalities and social acceptance of VAW. These aspects, though inadequate explanatory factors for VAW, point to the institutionalisation of violence in Kenya that allow for proliferation of violence supported by local cultural norms surrounding violence against women.

Given the discussion on VAW, we would argue that, as pointed out by scholars (Meintjes, Pillay and Turshen 2001; True 2012), the emphasis on addressing rights and material needs in the aftermath of conflicts tends to mask the reconstruction of patriarchal power despite recent emphasis on women's human rights. They point out that although both rights and needs are important for post-conflict reconstruction, neither is adequate either alone or in combination, for enabling women to realise substantive advancement because neither approach recognises the real need for social transformation (such as ending traditional gender restrictions) rather than the reconstruction of the past. True transformation encompasses addressing the gendered inequalities that are rooted in the structures and processes of the political economy of violence against women. This includes recognising women's social and reproductive roles and contributions, as well as their desires as sexual beings (Meintjes, Pillay and Turshen 2001; True 2012). In the absence of this recognition, these structural level forces continued to shape the physical experiences of violence for women and girls living in camps as the study findings have suggested.

CHAPTER FIVE

Responding to IDP Needs
The Twists, Turns and Rights

In the last two chapters, we have examined the experiences of internally displaced persons living in camps. We have noted how the social institutions in Kenya have largely failed to adequately provide basic human needs and services for persons living in camps. This structural violence shapes other forms of violence, such as intimate partner violence within families and the sexual exploitation of women and girls by persons in positions of power.

In this chapter, we turn to examine the humanitarian responses during and after the post-election conflicts. The aim of this chapter is not to critically examine all the responses, given the extent and the complexity of the responses. Rather, we aim to broadly highlight some of the response efforts in order to examine how they met the requirement for a human rights driven response for the post-election victims.

OVERVIEW OF HUMANITARIAN ASSISTANCE DURING AND AFTER THE ELECTION CONFLICTS

Immediately following the 2007-08 violent breakouts, there were a lot of humanitarian responses to people fleeing from violence. We must, however, appreciate that none of the actors involved were prepared for the extent and intensity of the violence and the resulting humanitarian emergency. For example, there was no clear policy and institutional framework for the initial coordination. Therefore, initial responses were unstructured and it became of immediate necessity to have some well-coordinated response mechanisms in order to ensure that all people fleeing from violence were well protected, and services were provided in a timely manner. Khassim Diagne of the UNHCR's Division of International Protection Services in a report on lessons learnt by UNHCR in the Kenyan crisis response pointed out that:

> The magnitude and the consequences of the displacement took the Government by surprise . . . Humanitarian agencies were equally not prepared, limited contingency planning had been put together to anticipate the scale and scope of the displacement. UNHCR was put at a particular disadvantage since the Office had no prior humanitarian activities regarding IDPs in Kenya before January 2008 and moreover, its refugee operations are located in an area of the country that experienced limited internal displacements (2008: 2).

Khassim further notes that this initial response was built in the form of a triangular approach where the Government through the Ministry of Special Programmes in the Office of the President, convened regular meetings with the UN Resident Coordinator and the Kenya Red Cross (KRC). This culminated in the creation of a National Disaster Operations Centre (NDOC) established to organise and coordinate the relief efforts with the KRC (Khassim 2008).[13] The Kenya Red Cross Society, as the lead implementing agency, was in charge of relief operations on behalf of the government especially focusing on the management and coordination of the camps. The UN agencies, on the other hand, employed the cluster approach.

According to the UN Office for the Coordination of Humanitarian Affairs (OCHA), clusters are groups of humanitarian organisations (UN and non-UN) working in the main sectors of humanitarian action such as shelter and health. They are created when clear humanitarian needs exist within a sector, when there are numerous actors within sectors and when national authorities need coordination support. The clusters serve to provide a clear point of contact and are accountable for adequate and appropriate humanitarian assistance. Additionally, they create partnerships between international humanitarian actors, national and local authorities, and civil society. On 9 January 2008, the cluster approach was activated and provided the framework for coordination for the international community's relief efforts.

In line with the cluster approach, each cluster was designated its own leadership, although some were co-chaired by different agencies. Kenya Red Cross was responsible for overall coordination. The clusters for example included the protection cluster led by UNHCR under which there were various sub-clusters such as the gender based violence (GBV) sub-cluster whose coordination was chaired by the UN Population Fund (UNFPA). Thus activating the cluster approach ensured that response efforts by all the various organisations and agencies were well coordinated. The government established a Mitigation and Resettlement Department in the Ministry of Special Programmes which allowed the humanitarian community to have a single entry, thereby enhancing the structure of coordination. Khassim, however, points out that there were questions raised as to "why the cluster approach was rolled out in the context of a strong and assertive government structure, overwhelmed by crisis but at no time dysfunctional."

In general, each of the clusters had a budget for its activities but the global appeal for funds did not realise the budget set. Therefore, while key decisions had been made and action taken to respond to the immediate survival needs of IDPs, there was a general air of uncertainty regarding the provision of aid. Additionally, the clusters had varied responses which had different impact for the welfare of the IDPs. For example, according to the WCRWC (2008:6), whereas the GBV sub-cluster seemed well coordinated and active,

> the RH (Reproductive Health) coordination, on the other hand, was lacking at all levels. While Health and Nutrition Cluster meetings were instituted in the inter-agency response, at the time of the assessment, Health Cluster coordination appeared to be less prioritised at the national level, with meetings postponed and cancelled without warning. At the field level where such meetings took place, a District RH Coordinator lamented that RH was peripheral.

Additionally, the report cites a lack of capacity in the Ministry of Health, Division of Reproductive Health to spearhead RH coordination in an acute emergency. Other challenges noted include lack of prioritisation of some needs such as reproductive health during emergency response, coordination meeting fatigue, lack of monetary resources for transportation, inadequate human resource and office supplies in the ministries. Furthermore, there were inadequate local coordination mechanisms resulting in delay in assistance.

Other challenges stemmed from some of the organisations viz. *Médecins Sans Frontières* and the International Committee of the Red Cross are not part of the cluster approach. This implies that they had their own parallel operations, even though they did share their data and activities with the cluster (IRIN 2008). Additionally, reports have indicated that some NGOs did not want to be associated with the UN, feeling that they would lose their independence. These challenges, including the fact that government had its own parallel response too, fragmented the efforts to adequately meet the welfare and dignity of IDPs as observed by a commissioner with the Kenya National Commission on Human Rights (IRIN 2008). At the same time, there were plans to begin the resettlement of IDPs.

THE RESETTLEMENT PROGRAMME POLITICS, BUREAUCRACY AND DIGNITY

In May 2008, the government of Kenya began the IDP resettlement process, dubbed as "Operation Rudi Nyumbani" (Return Home). By this time humanitarian agencies had begun pulling out their operations due to lack of funding and dwindling international attention to the plight of the internally displaced. Additionally, the government had intentions to cut down humanitarian assistance in order to 'facilitate' the resettlement exercise, in other words, to make IDPs leave the camps. On 5 May 2008, the first IDPs were taken back home. The military was present to transport and protect those who were willing to go back home.

Prior to the IDPs returning to their homes, according to the then Ministry of Special Programmes, the government gave 25,000 KSh (Kenyan shillings, equivalent to approximately USD 290) to the IDPs whose houses were burnt or destroyed and 10, 000 KSh (Kenyan shillings, equivalent to approximately USD 118) to those whose homes were looted. This money was supposed to help them restart their lives once again. The programme had several other components: increasing physical security (for example, the government constructed 30 new police posts); rehabilitate key services (rebuilt destroyed schools, clinics, markets and bridges) provide IDPs with assistance for the first three months of return (food, seeds, fertiliser and farm tools to restart livelihoods) and engage in peace and reconciliation activities with the host communities to put an end to inter-ethnic tensions (Kamungi 2011).

There were, however, many concerns by IDPs and various activists that the resettlement exercise was not adequately conceived. One of the most significant challenges was that the IDPs were still apprehensive about returning home despite government assurance of protection. They wondered how only five months after the evictions by their host communities, they would be assured of adequate security. Secondly, they openly, including through media, indicated that the money was too little to help them return home. In fact, in the 2008 data collection excise, some participants pointed out that some male IDPs had used the money to buy alcohol because they felt like it was "a slap in the face" compared to the property they had lost. Generally, there were concerns over the framework of resettlement. Kenya relied on the UN Guiding Principles on Internal Displacement but human rights activists criticised the government for ad-hoc application and violation of the UNGPID and failure to apply the Great Lakes Protocol.[14] These weaknesses in the structure of resettlement led to the satellite and self-help camps that we discussed earlier.

Overall, it seemed that the ORN was not as successful as the government had envisioned it to be. It mainly served to uproot the "humanitarian crisis" from the original camps and plant it in the various camps that subsequently mushroomed. In addition, there was no humanitarian intervention, as such, in these camps. With continued activism and highlighting of the IDP crisis, it became clearer to the government that some of the IDPs could not return home and needed resettlement land. Consequently, began the politics of purchasing land to resettle the IDPs.

The resettlement process was marked by political interference, conflicts and red tape slowing down the process of reconstructing IDPs livelihoods. For example, the lack of an IDP policy created conflicts between the Ministry of Special programmes and the Ministry of Lands in regard to management of funds for the purchase of resettlement land (Refugee Consortium of Kenya and Danish Refugee Council 2013). What this means is that as the conflicts of interests went on in the political circles, the IDPs continued to live in deplorable conditions in the camps. Yet, these conditions in turn shape other forms of violence within the families in the camps.

Both civil society organisations and media have constantly highlighted tension and differences of opinion between government and politicians or amongst politicians on how and where to resettle the IDPs. The Minister for Special Programmes, Esther Murugi, once pointed out in her press briefings that bad politics had slowed down the resettlement exercise. Further, the procurement process within the government departments complicated the efforts towards addressing the IDPs' problems. This slow-down process in the structures of government delayed the resettlement endeavours and as a result, IDPs had to bear human rights abuses in the camps. A senior government staff, Paulo, narrated to us the various dimensions of political challenges that played out in the resettlement exercise:

> One of the biggest problems that we have as the government is politicisation of the whole process. Okay, in as much as the process was genuine, politicians have taken advantage of this to castigate the government. They use it to look for votes or they use that to go and tell their communities that they are disadvantaged; why is this other community being favoured? You know that politicisation sometimes has even affected the rate at which we are buying land because we get a piece of land somewhere and the government cannot buy it because of politicisation and other issues that are brought by host communities against the resettlement. So, politicisation is a major issue.

As illustrated in the above excerpt, ethnic politics derail efforts in resettling IDPs. Politicians were severally accused of inciting their constituents not to accept resettlement of IDPs in their community. This happened particularly in places where some members of the community have less land than that to be allocated to the post-election conflict survivors or where there were other people who had been displaced or evicted from government land and forest reserves but had not been given land by the government yet. They wondered why the government should prioritise post-election conflict survivors over them. For example, Paulo told us they had to resettle some forest evictees before they could resettle the PEV victims because the politicians from the affected region had demanded it. Such resistance and conflicts were genuine and remind us of the deep structural problems of dealing with land equity and redistribution in Kenya. What the PEV crisis did, in this instance, was to highlight these weaknesses of the government.

Another challenge for the government was the stratification of IDPs. Kenyans of varying socio-economic classes were displaced during the election conflicts. This affected the ways in which different people coped with the conflicts. Some of the IDPs, like those with formal jobs in institutions such as education and health were able to get transfers and resume work after calm returned to the country. Others who had better financial resources before the conflicts left the camps in a much shorter period and restarted their lives anew. Still, others were lucky to have relatives who could host them and did not go to camps at all. The government refers to the IDPs who did not flee to a camp or left the camp by their own effort as 'integrated IDPs'. Those who stayed in the camps were referred to as the 'genuine' IDPs. Part of the tensions between the government and the human rights organisations has been due to the neglect of integrated IDPs by the government in the resettlement process. The government has argued that there is no way to certify that these integrated IDPs were actually affected by the post-election conflicts. To some government officials, these were people trying to take advantage so that they can get free land from the government. The government, therefore, only considers those labelled as 'genuine' IDPs in the resettlement process. Our intent is not to argue who is genuine or not, but to point out that this stratification had consequences for people's lives and access to basic needs.

Numerous non-governmental agencies/organisations, and independent commissions[15] have recommended reforms to ensure justice and restoration of livelihoods for the PEV victims but there has been a general lack of political will to address the problem. What is, hence, significant is the effect of these politics and government inadequacy on the various forms of violence that IDPs continue to experience in the camps. Specifically, the displaced men and women's bodies became the ground on which structural failures and political battles played out.

FUNDING FOR GENDER-BASED VIOLENCE PROGRAMMES

We have noted that the humanitarian assistance adopted the UN cluster approach. One of the clusters was Protection, led by UNHCR. This cluster had two sub-clusters: Child Protection and Gender-Based Violence. Like all other clusters, it constituted of government, civil society organisations and UN agencies. According to the Kenya National Commission on Human Rights (KNCHR) website, in early 2009, the Protection cluster transitioned into a national Protection Working Group on Internal Displacement (PWGID) chaired by the government departments – Ministry of Justice, National Cohesion and Constitutional Affairs and the KNCHR. The transition was necessary in order to expand its capacity for advocacy, address the needs of all displaced persons in Kenya and cover other interventions on a long term basis (KNCHR 2011; Refugee Consortium of Kenya and Danish Refugee Council 2013). The PWGID has field based protection working groups covering issues in gender-based violence, child protection and advocacy. Among its key achievements are acting as a coordination forum between state and non-state actors, therefore, giving prominence and visibility to IDP issues; advocating for long term solutions to internal displacement in Kenya and supporting the development of the IDP policy. On the other hand, the PWGID faced challenges with local level participation, national coordination of its mandate and limited financial resources and bureaucratic procedures that ultimately affected their implementations.[16] For example, during one of our visits to a research site in 2012, a senior official from the Ministry of Gender, Anita, noted that the GBV working group which is mainly involved in community sensitisation on gender violence, provision of psychosocial support for survivors of violence, advocacy for education of young girls, and provision of antiretroviral drugs for IDPs faced funding problems:

> We have our GBV working group which is being coordinated by this office and we have several members, quite a number of them being NGOs, CBOs, FBOs and government ministries like Ministry of Justice. We have some from the children's department, police department, all those who are dealing with issues of gender based violence. So we have actually that. . . we are not really funded, we just do our own fund raising and we reach out to communities and estates . . . whether they are in the camp or not, we manage to reach them and sensitise them on gender based violence issues. So we are working very closely with the civil society organisations.

This quote from a senior official questions government's commitment to funding GBV: the provincial administration chairs and coordinates the working group, yet the government provides inadequate funding for GBV programmes. Moreover, an officer from the gender unit at the local police station also decried underfunding by government. This apparent discrepancy in government's commitment to address gender violence raised concerns over the political will to end violence and protect the rights of women and girls as enshrined in human rights protocols. It is also important to point out that literature suggests that governments and states play a role in shaping gender relations through their various institutions and functions. For instance, Brush (2003) has noted that states are not gender neutral and treat women and men unequally, for example, through exclusion of women from citizenship. State social policies and practices have also privileged men as heads of household with women occupying a subordinate status. These have consequences for gender violence.

Further, on the issue of funding, the current President and his Deputy elected in March 2013 committed themselves to forming a lean, efficient government to cut costs. This process entailed reducing the number of ministries. In the new cabinet structure, there is no specific ministry in charge of gender. Instead, all ministries are expected to have a gender unit. A group of women legislatures[17] urged the president and his deputy to reconsider scraping the ministry. They argued that having gender units instead of full ministries would not attract as much funding on gender and noted the lack of political will in addressing gender issues. Kenya has a National Commission on Gender and Equality but according to one of the female[18] members of the Parliament, commissions do not have an implementation mandate. They can advise, recommend, investigate, oversee but they cannot implement as that is the mandate of the executive and cabinet. Furthermore, she notes that because Kenya is now living in a devolved democracy, "what is happening at the national level is being replicated at the county levels, so county governments have also omitted gender". These women leaders argue that the scraping of the ministry of gender will have set back in the gains so far made on gender equality and fighting gender-based violence. This, again raises questions regarding the government's commitment to the gender agenda.

WORKING RELATIONSHIP BETWEEN STATE AND HUMAN RIGHTS ORGANISATIONS

There are notable areas where the government has collaborated with non-governmental organisations and agencies on the issue of the IDPs. One of those was in the emergency response efforts following the violence. Both played crucial roles in the formation and coordination of clusters and sub clusters at both the national and field levels.

In addition, the development of the IDP policy was a multi-stakeholder, multi-sectoral process. On the other hand, challenges and tensions between the two groups surfaced in the interviews conducted with the representatives from both sides. Some human rights organisations accused the government of human rights violations, slow progress in resettlement and over emphasising resettlement over other human rights concerns in the camps. Conversely, one of the senior government officials we spoke with felt that these organisations, like the Human Rights Commission, were overly demanding yet the government had made every endeavour to ensure the resettlement of IDPs. For instance, when we asked Paulo whether and how they worked with the commission, he responded:

> Yes we do, a lot, they have their staff on the ground and we interact a lot on issues. But you see again our perspective as government and their perspective is not in tandem. If something happens, they want to come and tell the government "can you do this immediately?" Sometimes my hands will be tied . . . I have to talk to Nairobi. I have to write to Nairobi.

This tension is revealed further when human rights organisations ask that the government provides adequate food and other services to the IDPs as Paulo continued:

> You cannot satisfy everybody as a government. It's impossible, even the funds are not there. The prices of food have also escalated and the ministry of special programme's budget has remained the same. Therefore, providing the amount of food that is enough for everybody is not possible.

Noticeably, the 'lack of tandem' between government and organisations does little to end the experiences of violence in camps. Further, it points to lack of knowledge or ignorance of the myriad linkages between addressing political conflicts, provision of essential services and violence. This conceptualisation of violence as an isolated factor informs government's little attention to and funding for GBV programmes.

CONCLUDING THOUGHTS

In the last two chapters, we focused on life in camps whereas this chapter focuses on the responses to the crises. We found several gaps in the responses and in organising collective efforts across government and NGO responses – especially since these responses were meant to address or at least alleviate the challenges IDPs now faced. As we discussed the diverse responses by international agencies, NGOs and government, we pointed out the structural and cultural bottlenecks that stifle effective responses. We want to emphasise once again that our aim was not to extensively analyse the responses, along with the crises, but to highlight how the gaps in these responses, along with the structural problems in the government, negatively affect the dignity of the displaced persons.

CHAPTER SIX

Conclusion

Human Rights, Camp Life and Unanswered Questions

This book examines the lives of internally displaced persons after they have fled conditions of large-scale violence and sought shelters in the camps. We presented voices of some of the men and women living in the camps in order to highlight the core issues that shape their lives as internally displaced persons. A key emphasis of this book was to analyse the lived experiences of the women, men, girls and boys who fled the post-election violence in Kenya, as expressions of the historical and contemporary underlying social structural conditions. Even though the conflicts took an ethnic dimension, our analysis has not focused on an ethnic analysis of displacement. We have, however, taken a human rights perspective to examine the lives of displaced persons by way of analysing the larger structural conditions within which their individual and group lives are positioned. In this section, we offer a brief summary and concluding thoughts about what it means to live in the camps.

In chapter one, we provided an overview of the international and national human rights and the interactions between the two systems. We noted that human rights endeavour to achieve human dignity for all human beings. However, as we have noted, a major assumption of these standards is that people are located in a more stable context where they can access these rights. This vision of human rights begins to crumble when we examine vulnerable populations such as internally displaced persons living in camps. With that in mind, we turned to chapter two to provide a background on the socio-economic and political structural realities in Kenya. We looked at land inequalities. Land rights have been a major problem for Kenya. The history of land inequalities dates back to the colonial period. On politics, we looked at the pre-and post colonial period in Kenya. We examined how colonial politics have shaped present day socio-economic realities in Kenya. These politics are also tied to the rise of a political class that relies on militia gangs for political survival and power. Within these existing vulnerabilities, the rise of violent gangs – often employed by the influential functionaries to act against their opponents – further weakens the ability of marginalised persons to compose their lives in peaceful ways.

In chapter three, we turned to examine the lived realities of IDPs in camps. The purpose was to demonstrate how the social, economic and political structures that we presented in the chapter two shaped the lives of the displaced persons. Thus, we have highlighted the living conditions of IDPs: physical infrastructure and access to basic services such as water, sanitation, food and nutrition, health, security and education. We outlined how structural violence – built into the systems of the Kenyan society – deprives people of basic needs and resources that are critical to human development. It is a gross violation of human rights, which manifests in the powerlessness of the poor to reduce their suffering and to control their environment. We have argued that the failure to address various problems embedded in the Kenyan system – economic inequalities, provision of basic essentials, culture of violence as manifested in the formation of gangs, gender inequalities and unequal power relationships between women and men and the creation of an effective and accessible justice systems – shaped the lives of the internally displaced persons languishing in camps. As the Kenyan case study has shown, people living in camps are particularly vulnerable to social, cultural or political rights violations. Woven in these are structural impediments to the realisation of their human rights.

In chapter four, we chose to focus on violence against women and young girls. This was in an attempt to shift our minds to consider violence as a continuum wherein the private and public lives of women are intricately linked. This analysis is helpful in understanding how fragmented interventions in addressing the living conditions in the camps shape women and young girls' physical experiences of violence. We highlighted how physical and sexual VAW within the camp is linked to poverty and economic marginalisation, lack of basic services, cultural norms in Kenya that sponsor violence and inadequate justice systems. In chapter five, we turned to the efforts of international agencies, NGOs and government in trying to address different aspects of the lives of the IDPs. We highlighted the UN cluster approach to the humanitarian response and presented some specific challenges by the approach. We have noted that the response efforts were fragmented. We described the life of a young girl in the camp who is affected by hunger and poor nutrition, inadequate shelter and has no access to education: she is very susceptible to sexual exploitation. We showed that if interventions are fragmented – addressing only certain aspects of an individual's life – they do not fundamentally address the structural conditions to eliminate their vulnerability to violence.

When we reflect on the histories of Kenya, the election conflicts, the stories of the IDPs and the responses thereafter, what do they tell us? What really needs to happen? In this chapter, we address several questions that arise from our reflection on these issues. As we mentioned in the introduction, IDPs are a rapidly growing population as a result of wars, conflicts, natural and human-created disasters. Thus, the insights we provide in this book – about the conditions in camps that do not meet the minimal life standards expected by the human rights conventions of adequate housing, food, safety and other social aspects of life, violence that women and children face again, albeit in new forms – are particularly relevant.

Our identification of the gaps and inadequacies of response can be summarised as two major themes. First, that the conditions in the camps do not measure up to the standards being advocated by the UN Special Rapporteurs on adequate housing, food, water, education or health. Second, there is need to develop more integrated, sustained and effective responses to such monumental human crises.

A NOTE ON MEASURING VIOLENCE AGAINST WOMEN

We have noted that women and young girls, as nurturers and providers for their families, were particularly vulnerable to violence in the camps. We further noted that their vulnerability to this kind of violence is experienced in addition to the violence they originally fled. We have also discussed the factors that increase their vulnerability and some of the challenges in addressing violence against women in Kenya. Here, we would like to engage more with a broader issue that is a challenge to addressing violence against women.

Drawing upon the insights of this research, we argue that part of the problem in ending violence against women lies in the very definition and measurement of VAW. The Declaration on the Elimination of Violence against Women and other international human rights instruments adopted the concept of due diligence, in relation to violence against women, as a yardstick to assess whether the state has met its obligation. According to Ertürk (2006) under the due diligence obligation, states have a duty to take positive action to prevent and protect women from violence, punish perpetrators of violent acts and compensate victims of violence. But the application of due diligence standard has tended to be state-centric and limited to responding to violence when it occurs, largely neglecting the obligation to prevent and compensate, such as the state's duty to transform patriarchal structures and cultural values and norms that perpetuate VAW in the society. Further, the state-centric nature of due diligence fails to take into account the changing power dynamics and the challenges posed for state authority, and, therefore, calling into view the responsibility of non-state actors. For example, in the case of sexual exploitation and abuse by humanitarian workers, who should deal with the perpetrators?

In order to exercise due diligence, states are asked to promote research on the causes and consequences of VAW. To do this, there is a need for additional indicators to measure the violence. Measuring VAW is a complex issue given the multifaceted realities of different countries.[19] However, the general focus has been on measuring intimate partner violence because there are more data available on this and that IPV is the most common form of VAW. This approach[20] may be inaccurate given the under-researching of other forms of VAW. As Ertürk (2006) has argued, the mechanisms for measuring VAW as a continuum have been developed but these do not always shape policies at the level of the states. More pertinent to this case, the newest due diligence standards which include exactly the kind of vulnerabilities women experience in camps, are not actually used to measure violence in IDP camps. Thus, we raise an additional question: are states fully cognisant that current due diligence standards of VAW are actually meant to apply to IDP camps as well? As a corollary we ask, who defines VAW and who defines the types and severity of violence on the ground, who is responsible for due diligence in the camps? Should due diligence initiatives include measures to ensure the quality of the data and who should be charged with this type of oversight?

The most significant challenge with the current human rights legal frameworks is to ensure that the root causes and consequences of VAW are addressed at all levels, that is, from the private spheres of the home to the public spaces. States have dichotomised these two spheres and largely ignored the complexities of the interconnection of the spheres (Ertürk and Purkayastha 2012). Gender scholars have pointed out an integral link between private and public spheres of violence and clearly argued that the two cannot be separated, as has been the practice of state policies and institutions (Abraham 2000; Ertürk, 2008a; Ertürk and Purkayastha 2012; Ferree 1990; Sutton 2010). Ertürk and Purkayastha rightly note that there are a range of policies, institutional arrangements and practices that enable violence within private spheres, and that the "public/private codification in international law has for long served as an ideological barrier to the human rights system from responding to the violations of rights experienced by women in private life" (Ertürk and Purkayastha 2012: 45). Sutton (2010) adds that women's experience of violence in the family is not bound to be private but is critically related to material expressions of community and public space.

Turning our attention to the camps, we see that the conditions under which these women live constitute the conditions for occurrence of gender-based violence and are a gross violation of their rights. Evicted from their lands and businesses, these women bore the burden of production, reproduction and sheer survival in camps while they remained largely ignored by government whose main concern has been economic development and politics of succession. Women lived in deplorable conditions for over five years, with inadequate essential services. These circumstances shaped the various forms of violence experienced by women and girls within the camp. We must also understand this violence in the context of patriarchal hierarchies and other systems of subordination and inequality that create multiple layers of discrimination for women in order to effectively address VAW (Ertürk and Purkayastha 2012).

Over time, there has been, however, greater recognition of VAW in the camps by both government (especially the Ministry of Gender) and civil society, and there are endeavours to address such violence through encouraging reporting of perpetrators of violence, community sensitisation and education on gender violence. Nonetheless, these efforts must critically engage with structural level interventions, including challenging the enduring patriarchal domination of women, if we are to truly address the lives of displaced women. There is also massive pressure by civil society, especially national and international human rights organisations to protect the rights of IDPs, particularly women, and to help them reconstruct their livelihoods. Despite the tensions that exist between government and these organisations at times, these efforts need to be sustained at all levels in order to protect women's bodies from being the battleground for political supremacy.

The Government of Kenya has responsibility to protect displaced women in camps in light of the binding human rights commitments it has made both nationally and internationally, particularly in the recent National Policy on the Prevention of Internal Displacement and the Protection and Assistance to IDPs (IDP Bill) enacted by the Parliament in October 2012. This bill provides for a rights-based response to internal displacement; it gives full effect to the Great Lakes Protocol and the United Nations Guiding Principles on Internal Displacement. What is worth noting is that this IDP bill adopts the same principles in the UNGPID and GLP that were drawn upon in response efforts during and after the post-election conflicts, yet cases of VAW and other human rights violations have been rampant in camps. It is, therefore, doubtful that mere existence of a legal framework would create a difference for the lives of women and girls in the camps. There is an urgent need to move beyond the fragmented equality and justice approaches in responding to conflicts and forced migrations to challenging structures that shape gender to determine women and girls' secondary status in Kenya (Meintjes, Pillay and Turshen 2001).

UNANSWERED QUESTIONS AND THE RIGHTS OF IDPS

We have reflected on several issues in the process of writing this book, some of which we were not able to address within the ambit of this critique. This concluding note raises one key issue that, we think, requires immediate attention. In September 2013, the Kenyan government closed all the camps hosting IDPs affected by the 2007-08 post-election conflicts. Those IDPs who were not allocated land bought by the government, were instead given Ksh 400,000 either to buy the land themselves or start small businesses. Thus, by October 2013, officially there was no 2007-08 post-election violence IDPs. Ironically in mid-October 2013, a leading media house in Kenya (Standard) reported that some IDPs had returned to the camps citing that the government had failed to deliver construction materials for their houses. They also claimed that there were no amenities such as schools, hospitals or trading centres near the resettlement area, and as such, they had no food or water. During our interviews with human rights organisations representing IDPs, we had asked about the lives of IDPs after resettlement and the same issues of accessibility to basic amenities were raised.

In light of this, it is our view that closing camps or giving IDPs money to buy land on their own, or make other choices on livelihood reconstruction would not solve the problems we have discussed in this book. Without changing the structural conditions, the problems identified by the people quoted in this book are not going to be resolved or even mitigated. Moving people away from the IDP camps may just be the beginning of a whole new chapter of vulnerabilities that do not enable people to access human rights and build lives of human dignity. The camps may be closed but social circumstances developed in the camps envelop them wherever they may be resettled if adequate protection measures are not put in place. As a further project, we would suggest investigating how the human rights for the *resettled* IDPs are addressed.

References and Notes

Abudi, Michael, Felicia Yieke and Catherine Kitete. 2011. "The Discursive Constructions of Gender Among the Dholuo Speakers of Kenya" in *Living with Patriarchy: Discursive Constructions of Gendered Subjects Across Cultures,* edited by Danijela, Majstorovic and Inger Lassen. Netherlands: John Benjamins Publishing Co

Ardon, Patricia. 1999. *Post-War Reconstruction in Central America: Lessons from El Salvador, Guatemala, and Nicaragua*. Oxford: Oxfam Great Britain

Bassadien, Rasool S. and Tessa Hochfeld. 2005. "Across the Public/ Private Boundary: Contextualizing Domestic Violence in South Africa" *Agenda* 1 (1): 4-15

Bennett, Jane. 2005. "An Old Rag: South African Research on GBV and Debates on Culture and Rights" *Agenda* 24-35

Bop, Coudou. 2002. "Women in Conflicts, Their Gains and Their Losses" in *The Aftermath: Women in Post-Conflict Transformation,* edited by Meintjes, Sheila, Anu Pillay and Meredith Turshen. London and New York: Zed Books

Britton, Hanna. 2006. "Organizing against Gender Violence in South Africa" in *Journal of South African Studies* 32(1): 145-163

Brush, Lisa. 2003. *Gender and Governance*. Walnut Creek, CA: Altamira Press

Bunch, Charlotte. 1995. "Transforming Human Rights from a Feminist Perspective" in *Women's Rights, Human Rights: International Feminist Perspectives,* edited by J. Peters and A. Wolper. New York: Routledge

Bunutu-Gomez, Michael Ba. 2011. *Global Leadership Change, Organizations, and Development*. Bloomington: Universe

Center for Reproductive Rights and Federation of Women Lawyers-Kenya. 2008. *At Risk: Rights Violations of HIV-Positive Women in Kenyan Health Facilities*. New York: Centre for Reproductive Rights

Center for Rights and Education Awareness. 2008. *Women Paid the Price: A Report on Sexual and Gender Based Violence in the 2007 Post-Election Conflicts in Kenya*. Nairobi, Kenya: Centre for Rights, Education and Awareness

Dorina, Bekoe. 2012. *Voting in Fear: Electoral Violence in Sub-Saharan Africa*. Washington DC: United State Institute of Peace

Dukes, E. Franklin. 1999. "Structural Forces in Conflict and Conflict Resolution in Democratic Society" in *Conflict Resolution: Dynamics, Process, and Structure*, edited by Ho-Won Jeong. Vermont: Ashgate Publishing Co

Eriksson-Baaz, Maria and Maria Stern. 2013. *Sexual Violence as a Weapon of War? Perceptions, Prescriptions, Problems in the Congo and Beyond*. London and New York: Zed Books

Erin Mooney. 2002. "The Concept of Internal Displacement and the Case for Internally Displaced Persons as a Category of Concern" in *Refugee Survey Quarterly*. 24 (3)

Ertürk, Yakýn and Bandana Purkayastha. 2012. "Linking Research, Policy and Action: A Look at the Work of the Special Rapporteur on Violence Against Women" in *Current Sociology* 60(2): 142–160

Ertürk, Yakin. 2008b. UN Human Rights Council, Report of the Special Rapporteur on Violence Against Women, its Causes and Consequences, Indicators on Violence against Women and State Response, 29 January 2008, A/HRC/7/6. Retrieved 18 September 2013 (http://www.refworld.org/docid/47cd6c442.html).

Ertürk, Yakin. 2006. UN Commission on Human Rights, Report of the Special Rapporteur on Violence against Women, its Causes and Consequences, to the Due Diligence Standards as a Tool for the Elimination of Violence against Women, 20 January 2006 E/CN.4/2006/61. Retrieved 18 September 2013. (http://www.refworld.org/pdfid/45377afb0.pdf)

Federation of Women Layers-Kenya. 2002. "Domestic Violence in Kenya: A Report of a baseline Survey among Women in Nairobi." Nairobi, Kenya: FIDA.

Ferree, Myra M. 1990. "Beyond Separate Spheres" in *Journal of Marriage and Family* (52): 866-887.

Francis, Elizabeth. 1995. "Migration and Changing Divisions of Labor: Gender Relations and Economic Change in Koguta, Western Kenya" *Africa* 65(2): 197-216.

Gruskin, Sofia, Michael A. Grodin, George J. Annas and Stephen P. Marks. Eds. 2005. *Perspectives on Health and Human Rights*. New York: Routledge.

Government of Kenya. 2008. *Report of the Commission of Inquiry into Post-Election Violence (CIPEV)*. Government Printer. Nairobi, Kenya.

Government of Kenya. 2012. *Internally Displaced Persons Bill 2012*. Nairobi, Kenya: Kenya Law Reports. Retrieved 4 February 2013 (http://www.kenyalaw.org/klr/index.php?id=949).

Grant, Stefanie. 2005. *Migrants' Human Rights: From the Margins to the Mainstream*. Migration Information Source. Retrieved 1 September 2013. (http://www.migrationinformation.org/Feature/display.cfm?id=291).

Giles Wenona, Mary and Hyndman Jennifer. Eds. 2004. *Sites of Violence: Gender and Conflict Zones*. CA: University of California Press.

Harbeson, J. 1973. *Nation-building in Kenya: The Role of Land Reform*. Evanston, IL: Northwestern University Press.

Hornsby, Charles. 2012. *Kenya: A History Since Independence*. New York: I. B. Tauris & Co Ltd

Human Rights Committee. 2010. Consideration of Reports Submitted by States Parties under Article 40 of the Covenant. Third Periodic Report of States Parties, Kenya. Geneva: UN Human Rights Council.

Human Rights Watch. 2011. *Turning Pebbles: Evading Accountability for Post-Election Violence in Kenya*. Retrieved 13 September 2013 (http://www.hrw.org/sites/default/files/reports/kenya1211webwcover_0.pdf).

Internal Displacement Monitoring Centre. 2012. *Global Overview 2011: People Displaced by Conflict and Violence*. IDPMC and NRC. Retrieved 26 April 2013 (http://www.unhcr.org/50f95f7a9.html).

International Labour Organization and Kenya National Bureau of Statistics 2012. *Kenya Child Labour Baseline Survey: Busia District Report*. Nairobi, Kenya. Retrieved 14 May 2013 (www.ilo.org/ipec).

Internal Displacement Monitoring Centre. 2012. *IDP's Significant Needs Remain as Inter-Communal Violence Increases*. Geneva, Switzerland: Norwegian Refugee Council. Retrieved 12 September 2013 (www.internal-displacement.org).

Internal Displacement Monitoring Centre. 2007. *Internal Displacement: Global Overview of Trends and Developments in 2006*. Geneva, Switzerland: Norwegian Refugee Council. Retrieved 19 November 2013 (www.internal-displacement.org).

Ishay, Micheline R. 2004. "What are Human Rights: Six historical Controversies" in *Journal of Human Rights* 3 (3): 359-371

Kälin, Walter. 2010. The Human Rights of Internally Displaced Persons. Speech by the Representative of the Secretary-General on the Human Rights of Internally Displaced Persons presented to the United Nations Human Rights Council, 8 March 2010.

Kamungi, P. 2009. "What Pact, What Protocol? The Irrelevance of the Great Lakes Protocols in Responding to Kenya's Post-Election Humanitarian Crisis". Paper presented at the London School of

Economics, May 2009

Kamungi, P. and Klopp J. 2007. "Failure to Protect: Lessons from Kenya's IDP Network". *Forced Migration Review,* 53: 58

Kanyinga, Karuti. 1998. The Land Question in Kenya: Struggles, Accumulation and Changing Politics. PhD Dissertation, Netherlands: Roskilde University

Kanyinga, Karuti. 2009. The Legacy of the White Highlands: Land Rights, Ethnicity, and Post-2007 Election Violence in Kenya. *Journal of Contemporary African Studies* (27) 3:325-344

Khassim, Diagne. 2008. *Lessons Learned from UNHCR'S Emergency Operation for Internally Displaced Persons in Kenya. Division of International Protection Services*. Geneva, Switzerland: UNHCR. Retrieved 19 October 2013 (http://www.unhcr.org/48e5d90d2.html).

Kenya Human Rights Commission. 2009. *Out in the Cold: The Fate of Internally Displaced Persons (2008-2009)*. Nairobi, Kenya: Kenya Human Rights Commission. Retrieved 30 July 2012 (http://www.khrc.or.ke)

Kenya Human Rights Commission. 2008. *A Tale of Force, Threats and Lies: Operation Rudi Nyumbani in Perspective*. Nairobi, Kenya: Kenya Human Rights Commission. Retrieved 30 July 2012 (http://www.khrc.or.ke)

Kenya National Bureau of Statistics and ICF Macro. 2010. *Kenya Demographic and Health Survey 2008-09*. Calverton, Maryland: KNBS and ICF Macro. Retrieved 2 March 2012, (http://statistics.knbs.or.ke/nada/index.php/catalog/23/download/75)

Klopp, J. 2001. "Ethnic land clashes and winning elections: The case of Kenya's Electoral Despotism" in *Canadian Journal of African Studies* 35 (3): 473-517

Kuria, Anthony. 2007. Human Rights, Social justice and Social Development in Kenya. Paper Presented at the 'Mijadala on Social Policy, Governance and Development in Kenya' sponsored by Development Policy Management Forum on 22 March 2007 at Nairobi Safari Club

Leo, C. 1989. *Land and class in Kenya*. Harare, Zimbabwe: Nehands

Lomo. A. Zachary. 2000. "The Struggle for Protection of the Rights of Refugees and IDPs in Africa: Making the Existing International Legal Regime Work" in *Berkeley Journal of International Law* 18 (2): 268-284

Maiese, Michelle. 2003. "Social Structural Change" in *Beyond Intractability*. Edited by Guy Burgess and Heidi Burgess. Conflict Research Consortium, University of Colorado, Boulder, Colorado, USA. Retrieved 17 November 2013 (http://www.beyondintractability.org/essay/social-structural-changes)

Majodina, Zonke. 2009. Protection, Human Rights and Forced Migration. Keynote Paper Present at the International Conference: "Protecting

People in Conflict and Crisis: Responding to the Challenges of a Changing World". September 2009. Refugee Studies Centre. University of Oxford

McKay, Susan. 1998. "The Effects of Armed conflict on Girls and Women" in *Journal of Peace Psychology* 4(4): 381-392

McKenzie, F. 1990. "Gender and Land Rights in Murang'a District, Kenya" in *Journal of Peasant Studies* 17(4): 609-43

Meintjes, Sheila, Anu Pillay and Meredith Turshen. Eds. 2002. *The Aftermath: Women in Post-Conflict Transformation*. London and New York: Zed Books

Moser .O.N. Caroline and Fiona Clark. Eds. 2001. *Victims, Perpetrators or Actors? Gender, Armed Conflict and Political Violence*. London: Zed Books.

Merry, Sally E. 2006. *Human Rights and Gender Violence: Translating International Law into Local Justice*. Chicago: University of Chicago Press

Ngwacho, Areba, Paul Ondimm, Esther Monga're and Zablon Nyakundi. 2013. "The Hidden Costs of Free Primary Education and Their Implication on Enrolment in Kisii Central District, Kenya" in *Journal of Education and Practice*. 4 (18): 97-106

Njeru, Enos H. N. and John Orodho. 2003. Education Financing in Kenya: Secondary School Bursary Scheme Implementation and Challenges. In Discussion IPAR Discussion Paper Series No.035/2003. Nairobi, Kenya

Okoth-Ogendo, W. 1981. "Land Ownership and Land Distribution in Kenya's Large Farm Areas" in *Papers on the Kenyan economy: Performance, Problems and Policies,* edited by T. Killick. London: Heinemann

Omara-Otunnu, Amii, Purkayastha, Bandana and Mobilia, Sergio. Eds. 2012. Human Rights: Voices of the World's Young Activists. London: Frontpage Publications

Ombwori, Fredrick. 2009. Status of Gender Desks at Police Stations in Kenya. A Case Study of Nairobi Province. A Research Series No. 22. September 2009. Institute of Economic Affairs, Nairobi, Kenya

Oloo Adams. 2010. "Marginalization and the Rise of Militia Groups in Kenya; The Mungiki and the Sabaot Land Defence Force" in *Militias, Rebels and Islamist Militants. Human Insecurity and State Crisis in Africa*, Eds. Adams Oloo, Wafula Okumu and Augustine Ikelegbe. South Africa

Phuong Catherine. 2000. "Internally Displaced Persons And Refugees: Conceptual Differences And Similarities" in *Netherlands Quarterly Of Human Rights*. Vol. 18 (2): 215-22

Phuong, Catherine. 2004. *The International Protection of Internally Displaced Persons*. Cambridge University Press

Prescott, Jordan and Adrian Madsen. Eds. 2011. *Sexual Violence in Africa's*

Conflict Zones. Nova Science Publishers Inc

Ray, Ranita and Purkayastha Bandana. 2012. "Challenges in Localizing Global Human Rights" in *Societies without Borders* (7): 29-51

Refugee Consortium of Kenya and Danish Refugee Council. 2013. Behind the Scenes: Lessons Learnt from Developing a National Policy Framework on Internal Displacement in Kenya. Nairobi, Kenya.

Rubenstein. E. Richard. 1999. "Conflict Resolution and the Structural Sources of Conflict" in *Conflict Resolution: Dynamics, Process, and Structure, edited by* Ho-Won Jeong. Vermont: Ashgate Publishing Co

Sutton, Barbara. 2010. *Bodies in Crisis: Culture, Violence and Women's Resistance in Neoliberal Argentina*. New Brunswick, NJ: Rutgers University Press

Swamy, Gurushi. 1994. "Kenya: Structural Adjustment in the 1980s" World Bank Policy Research Working Paper 1238. Washington, DC: World Bank

Throup, D. 2008. "The count" in *Journal of Eastern Africa Studies* 2 (2): 290-304

Turshen Meintjes. 2001. "The Political Economy of Rape: An Analysis of Systematic Rape and Sexual Abuse of Women During Armed Conflict in Africa" in *Gender, Armed Conflict and Political Violence*, Eds. Moser and Frank. London: Zed Books

Turshen Meintjes and C. Twagiramariya. Eds. 1998. *What Women Do in Wartime: Gender and Conflict in Africa*. London and New York: Zed Books

UN High Commission for Refugees. 2013. *On the Run in their Own Land*. Retrieved 30 March 2013 (http://www.unhcr.org/pages/49c3646c146.html).

United Nations (2013). Universal Declaration of Human Rights. Retrieved 20 February 2013 (http://www.un.org/en/documents/udhr/).

UN Office of the Commissioner for Human Rights. 2008. Report of Fact Finding Mission to Kenya. 6-28 February 2008.

US Department of State. 2012. Kenya Profile. Retrieved 10 December 2013 (http://www.state.gov/outofdate/bgn/kenya/201469.html).

Wanyeki Muthoni. 2008. "Lessons from Kenya: Women and Post-Election Violence" pp.91-97 in *Militarism, Conflict and Women's Activism*, Eds. A. Mama and M. Okazawa-Rey. *Feminist Africa*. Issue 10. Africa Gender Institute, University of Cape Town, South Africa

Wily, L. 2006. *Land Rights Reform and Governance in Africa*. Nairobi: United Nations Development Programme

Winter, Deborah D. and Dana C. Leighton. 2001. "Structural Violence" in *Peace, Conflict, and Violence: Peace Psychology in the 21st Century*, Eds. D. J. Christie, R. V. Wagner and D. D. Winter. New York: Prentice-Hall

Women's Commission for Refugee Women and Children. 2008. Reproductive Health Coordination Gap, Services Ad hoc: Minimum Initial Service Package (MISP) Assessment in Kenya. Retrieved 21 November 2013 (http://reliefweb.int/report/kenya/reproductive-health-coordination-gap-services-ad-hoc-minimum-initial-service-package).

NEWSPAPER ARTICLES

Gitonga, Antony. 2013. IDPs Return to Naivasha Camp, Say State has abandoned them. The Standard Newspaper, Kenya. 18 October 2013

Kareithi, Amos. 2008. "Rains, Food Shortage add misery to IDPs" in East African Standard. 31 March 2008

WEB RESOURCES

Article 19 .2013. Kenya: Law to Protect Internally Displaced People Enacted Ahead of Election http://www.article19.org/resources.php/resource/3625/en/kenya:-law-to-protect-internally-displaced-people-enacted-ahead-of-election Retrieved 4 June 2012

Antony Gitonga. 2013. IDPs Return to Naivasha Camp, Say State has abandoned them. *The Standard Newspaper* Kenya. 18 October 2013

East African Standard. 31 March 2008

NOTES

1 The 1951 Convention Relating to the Status of Refugees defines a refugee as, "any person who is outside their country of origin and unable or unwilling to return there or to avail themselves of its protection, on account of a well-founded fear of persecution for reasons of race, religion, nationality, membership of a particular group, or political opinion. Stateless persons may also be refugees in this sense, where country of origin (citizenship) is understood as 'country of former habitual residence'. Those who possess more than one nationality will only be considered as refugees within the Convention if such other nationality or nationalities are ineffective (that is, do not provide protection)".

2 For a more comprehensive analysis of the conceptual challenges with this initial definition of IDPs, see Mooney (2005).

3 The 1951 Convention Relating to the Status of Refugees defines a refugee as, "any person who is outside their country of origin and unable or unwilling to return there or to avail themselves of its

protection, on account of a well-founded fear of persecution for reasons of race, religion, nationality, membership of a particular group, or political opinion. Stateless persons may also be refugees in this sense, where country of origin (citizenship) is understood as 'country of former habitual residence'. Those who possess more than one nationality will only be considered as refugees within the Convention if such other nationality or nationalities are ineffective (that is, do not provide protection)".

A more comprehensive discussion on conceptual differences and similarities between refugees and IDPs is found in Catherine Phuong's book: The International protection of Internally Displaced Persons (2004)

4 Countries in the African Great Lakes region include Burundi, the Democratic Republic of Congo, Kenya, Rwanda, Tanzania and Uganda

5 In all ethnic political violence, the Rift Valley region is significant in Kenya's national politics for several reasons. First, it is a multi-ethnic region with several ethnic groups settled in the province. Numerically significant groups include the Kalenjin, Maasai, Kikuyu, and Luyha. The Kalenjin are the largest group, comprising about half of the total population. Second, the region has the largest share of total national votes and parliamentary constituencies, making it attractive because of the share of total national votes and parliamentary seats that parties can obtain from the ethnic blocs in the area. Third, most of the former white highlands are in the Rift Valley. Various groups have been competing to gain secure land rights in the highlands. Ethnicity has been central in this competition, and the post-2007 political conflict has its roots in this dimension (Kanyinga 2009).

6 Many Kikuyus who settled in the Rift Valley region, predominantly occupied by the Kalenjin and Maasai, have used Kikuyu names to call their zones of settlements. In some cases, these areas are given the same names as those of the areas where the Kikuyu settlers originated, the Central region of Kenya.

7 Kanyinga (2009) points out that because Moi had completed his constitutionally permitted terms in office, there was no pressure on the Kalenjin elite to fight for him. Additionally, Moi had identified Uhuru Kenyatta, a Kikuyu, as KANU's candidate for the presidency. This strategy conflated Kikuyu-Kalenjin elite interests. Uhuru Kenyatta would protect Moi's and the Kalenjin interests when the former retired from political life, and the Kikuyu interests would be safeguarded under a Kikuyu presidency and KANU leadership.

8 See the KNDR agenda 2: Immediate measures to address the humanitarian crisis, promote reconciliation, and healing.

9 See the Kenya Human Rights Commission. 2009. "Out in the Cold" page 19: IDP Resettlement: Force, Threats and Lies. This report discusses the rationale and assumptions for the resettlement programme.

10 Despite the government of Kenya's efforts to provide free and accessible primary education, close to four million children still remain out of school due to hidden costs (Census Report 2009). Studies show that these hidden costs include buying school uniforms, examination fees, development fee, activity fee and other miscellaneous fees. For more details see for example Ngwacho et al (2013).

11. There is a dearth of literature on the use of sexual violence or rape during wartime. See for example, Beverly Allen (1996), *Rape Warfare: The Hidden Genocide in Bosnia-Herzegovina and Croatia;* Leatherman Janie (2011), *Sexual Violence and Armed Conflict;* Jordan Prescott, Adrian M Madsen (2011), *Sexual Violence in Africa's Conflict Zones;* Weaver, Gina Marie (2010), *Ideologies of Forgetting: Rape in the Vietnam War.*

There is also an emerging literature that problematises the global governing discourse: "rape as a weapon of war". For a recent example see Eriksson Baaz and Stern (2013).

12 Some African scholarship has argued that the dichotomy private/ public sphere is based on a western liberal political philosophy and did not exist in that strict sense in Africa. Further, scholars such as Bassadien and Hochfeld (2005) have argued that violence does not occur behind closed doors and is thus not a private affair. Often those in the survivor's immediate environment are aware of the violence even if they do not actually witness it.

13 According to Khassim, this triangular approach had been created through an Act of Parliament in 1965 to "provide relief to victims of catastrophe or disasters" and offered the Government a good opportunity to deploy it in the worst affected areas while handling the problems of acceptability and legitimacy that government officials were facing.

14 See IRIN News, 16 October 2008 for reactions by some Human Rights activists

15 For references on specific recommendations see, for example, Commission of Inquiry into the Post-Election Violence (CIPEV) 2008; Kenya Human Rights Commission, 2009. Out in the Cold: The Fate of IDPs (2008-2009); Centre for Rights and Education Awareness, 2008. Women Paid the Price. A Report on Sexual and Gender Based Violence in the 2007 Post-Election Conflicts in Kenya; Human Rights Watch Report 2011; Turning Pebbles: Evading Accountability for PEV in Kenya.

16 For more on achievements and challenges, see the Refugee Consortium of Kenya and Danish Refugee Council 2013 study on Lessons Learnt from Developing a National Policy Framework on Internal Displacement in Kenya.

17 See the Kenya Star, Newspaper, 17 May 2013.

18 See blog by Priscilla Nyokabi, a member of Parliament – http://www.wakilinyokabi.com/my-blog/item/14-kenya-needs-the-ministry-of-gender-youth-and-child-development.

19 In 2004, the UN Special Rapporteur on VAW proposes the need to develop indices on measuring VAW and on state responses to it. Following this, there were numerous proposals across the UN agencies, regional bodies, governments and civil society organisations. The Office of the UN High Commissioner for Human Rights (OHCHR) also proposed human rights indicators.

20 This approach ignores the standards set in the 1993 Declaration and may be inaccurate given the under-researching of other forms of VAW and disjunctions between research and policy definitions of IPV in multiple cultural contexts.